MEXICO 2005
THE CHALLENGES OF
THE NEW MILLENNIUM

Significant Issues Series
Timely books presenting current CSIS research and analysis of interest to the academic, business, government, and policy communities.
Managing editor: Roberta L. Howard

■ ■ ■

The Center for Strategic and International Studies (CSIS), established in 1962, is a private, tax-exempt institution focusing on international public policy issues. Its research is nonpartisan and nonproprietary.

CSIS is dedicated to policy analysis and impact. It seeks to inform and shape selected policy decisions in government and the private sector to meet the increasingly complex and difficult global challenges that leaders will confront in the next century. It achieves this mission in three ways: by generating strategic analysis that is anticipatory and interdisciplinary; by convening policymakers and other influential parties to assess key issues; and by building structures for policy action.

CSIS does not take specific public policy positions. Accordingly, all views, positions, and conclusions expressed in this publication should be understood to be solely those of the author.

The CSIS Press
Center for Strategic and International Studies
1800 K Street, N.W.
Washington, D.C. 20006
Telephone: (202) 887-0200
Fax: (202) 775-3199
E-mail: books@csis.org Web site: http://www.csis.org/

MEXICO 2005
THE CHALLENGES OF
THE NEW MILLENNIUM

MICHAEL J. MAZARR

Foreword by Federico Reyes-Heroles

THE CSIS PRESS

Center for Strategic
and International Studies
Washington, D.C.

972.0836 M475m
Mazarr, Michael J., 1965-
Mexico 2005

The CSIS Press, Washington, D.C. 20006
©1999 by the Center for Strategic and International Studies
All rights reserved.
Printed on recycled paper in the United States of America
03 02 01 00 99   5 4 3 2

ISSN 0736-7136
ISBN 0-89206-338-6

All photographs, including the cover photo, by Larry Luxner and reproduced by permission.
Cover design by Robert L. Wiser, Archetype Press, Washington, D.C.

Library of Congress Cataloging-in-Publication Data

Mazarr, Michael J., 1965-
  Mexico 2005 : the challenges of the new millennium / Michael J. Mazarr : foreword by Federico Reyes-Heroles
    p. cm. — (Significant issues series. ISSN 0736-7163 : v. 21 no. 2)
  A CSIS global trends 2005 study.
  Includes bibliographical references (p.) an index.
  ISBN 0-89206-338-6
  1. Mexico—Civilization—20th century. 2. Mexico—Forecasting. 3. Twenty-first century—Forecasts. 4. Economic forecasting—Mexico. 5. Social prediction—Mexico. 6. Mexico—Social conditions—1970- 7. Mexico—Economic conditions—1994- 8. Mexico—Relations—Foreign countries. I. Reyes-Heroles, Federico. II. CSIS global trends 2005 study (United States) III. Title. IV. Series.
F1236.M395 1999   98-41066
972.08'36—dc21   CIP

Contents

List of Figures vi
Acknowledgments vii
Foreword ix
Introduction xv

1 Trend One: The Foundations 1

2 Trend Two: The Engines of History 29

3 Trend Three: A Human Resources Economy 45

4 Trend Four: An Era of Global Tribes 73

5 Trend Five: The Rise of New Authorities 93

6 Trend Six: A Test of Human Psychology 119

7 Scenarios for Mexico's Development 135

8 The Knowledge Era and Mexico 165

Index 171
About the Author

Figures

1. World Population, 1950–2010   3
2. World Grain Production, 1950–1990   4
3. World Oil Prices, 1970–2010   6
4. Mexico's Population, 1960–2040   8
5. Mexico's Young but Aging Population, 1970–2010   9
6. Ultimately, An Old Population: Percentage of Population over 60, 1990–2075   12
7. Water Supply and Demand in the Valley of Mexico, 1990–2025   18
8. Mexico's Projected Oil Production, 1930–2080   20
9. Economic Freedom in the World, 1975–1995   33
10. The Advance of Democracy, 1800s–2005   34
11. Political Participation in Mexico, 1981–1990   37
12. Mexico's Open Economy: Trade Liberalization Index, 1989–1996   39
13. World Trade in Services, 1980–1993   46
14. The Rise of the Developing World   51
15. Mexico's Exports, 1995   53
16. Growth of Mexico's Exports and Foreign Direct Investment, 1980–1996   55
17. *Maquiladora* Growth: Numbers and Growth Rate of Employed Workers, 1994–1997   55
18. Mexico's Exports: Growth Rate and Share of World Exports   56
19. Overdue Loan Ratio, Commercial Banks, 1989–1996   61
20. Gross Domestic Savings Rate, 1990–1996   62
21. A Widening Gap: White- and Blue-Collar Real Hourly Wages, 1985–1995   64
22. World Trade Integration, 1972–2002   74
23. Postmaterialist Values in Mexico   81
24. Characteristics of Knowledge-Era Authorities   96
25. Americans' Perceptions of Broad Social Trends, 1988–1995   125

Acknowledgments

THE CSIS GLOBAL TRENDS 2005 PROJECT, of which this monograph is a part, aims to describe the challenges faced by individual countries, such as Mexico, and to unearth new ideas about those challenges by viewing the countries' prospects through the prism of broadly dispersed patterns and tendencies. While this methodology has proved useful, it also creates a dilemma. Given that those steeped in the general trends are not country specialists, and given that the country specialists may have at best a passing interest in the trends, who writes the book?

Our answer has differed from country to country. In this case we decided that the project director, informed by several months of research, would write the analysis. As the project director thus chosen, I must immediately acknowledge that I am not a specialist on Mexico and would never pretend to be one. To help me think through the issues, I have enlisted the support of a number of prominent Mexicanists in the United States working both inside and outside of government. Three of these advisers—Roderic Ai Camp, Miguel Centeno, and George Grayson—have been especially helpful, providing detailed analysis and reviewing drafts of the monograph. I owe each an immense debt of gratitude for contributing a number of insights and saving me from foolish errors. This being said, the final interpretation remains mine alone, and these three generous and expert scholars should not be held responsible for the contents of the volume.

I hope that other specialists will similarly forgive the intrusion by a generalist on their area of expertise and will perhaps even find some value in my efforts to illuminate the interactions between global and national trends. The aim of this country study, as of the overall project, is fairly modest. It does not attempt to furnish final answers or detailed forecasts for the trends that are changing the country. In the end I hope only that it asks the right questions and poses the right issues for future deliberation.

CSIS would like to extend warm thanks to the Rockefeller Brothers Fund for its keen interest in the Global Trends project and for the financial support that helped make it possible.

Foreword

According to Bertrand Russell, a characteristic feature of civilized societies is their ability to look ahead. A society that fails to plan in advance will always arrive late at the solution of its problems. This leads to asking why, if preventive measures are so beneficial, not all societies have adopted them. Today, close to the end of the century and the millennium, it could be said that, even more risky, the nations of the international community that conduct prospective exercises are an evident minority. Why is this? What is the obstacle?

Planning, or the serious and formal attempt to exert an impact on the future, is an ancient practice. Throughout history, great efforts have been devoted to analyzing the relationship between the ability to generate a surplus, basically agricultural, and the question of what to do with the resources and time thus liberated. The data and technologies used hundreds or even thousands of years ago were limited. Nonetheless, it is still amazing to realize how the rational consumption and use of water resulted in the construction of great hydraulic works, whether in Mesopotamia, in the Far East, or in Machu Picchu. These huge hydraulic works demanded an efficient organization of labor, clearly established hierarchies, and well-defined plans, and they are brilliant examples of how certain societies looked to the future.

Not all primitive societies or ancient civilizations that practiced planning in a certain field, however, considered this an ongoing activity, understood it as a way of ruling. Frequently, those in charge of planning, of looking into the future, served despotic or authoritarian regimes that did not socially institutionalize prospective studies. When planning plays power games, sooner or later it stumbles. The five-year plans of the Soviet Union are a monument to prospective exercises that lacked a social foundation.

Our question remains unanswered. What conditions are necessary if planning is to take root in a society? Technological progress, already mentioned, is only a partial explanation. Not all societies that have achieved scientific or technological brilliancy have at the same time implemented systematized planning and prospective actions. Their scientific attainments have been like shooting stars. Prospective studies must become a social demand as opposed to a scholarly pastime; they require systematic efforts and, consequently, certain links with power. It is thus necessary to look toward those social conditions that enable the thriving of attempts to attain a better knowledge of the future that will allow acting upon it.

The first issue, far from being as abstract and ethereal as it may seem, rests on the fact that not all societies yet agree that human action can and should modify the future. In countless religious concepts, the idea of the future, of divine fate, opposes the conception that human beings should influence their future as much as they are able. Thus a first condition for prospective studies could be called the secularization of the future. Turgot, as did all the other celebrated advocates of the idea of progress, certainly contributed toward this end.

How important is the weight of culture? During this turn of the century, when even World Bank studies point toward cultural variables as central to the advancement of economies, there can be no doubt that culture stands solid as a rock. The secularization of the future is still a goal of the greatly discussed globalized world. It is a first step.

Prospective studies also require great maturity among political actors. Many of the decisions that are made or must be made through the cold lens of prospective studies restrain the decisionmaking framework of parties and pressure groups. Thus, the fields of action of ideology and subjective social pressures are reduced. Technical knowledge and common sense must prevail. Unfounded fantasies or expectations must disappear. If decisions concerning the future become politicized, there is a risk of falling into cheap rhetoric.

The secularization of a field that refers to the future and the maturity of political parties and other actors are essential for the establishment of long-term state policies. Issues concerned with population, ecology, food production, and energy use, for example, cannot be made ineffective to suit individual moods. Prospective studies assume a minimum of overall, desirable, long-term agreements, goals, and objectives. This means that these instruments cannot be modified according to the particular view of each new congress or each incumbent of the executive. Prospective studies establish a more or less limited catalogue of what everyone should expect. It is not a matter of sheer deontology or what should be. Prospective studies are a mixture of expectations and reality.

This area of essential agreements reveals that the image of the nation-state is solid enough to withstand political oscillations. It reveals that there is thus a new authority that is beyond parties and their interests and that is widely accepted. One last point, equally important, is that no planning or serious exercises about the future are possible without true and reliable data. The information revolution has generated an enormous responsibility. Never before have humans handled a similar amount of data about the future, and they must do so responsibly.

The above are the minimum conditions under which prospective studies can thrive. Now we can understand the importance of this text on Mexico. This book belongs to the recent wave of research on the Mexican future that suggests that the country is entering a new and promising stage of discussion. Being able to talk about Mexican prospective studies is to admit there has been a gap in the national discussion. It concerns Mexicans and people abroad. Fewer myths, more facts. According to Octavio Paz, the United States is a country of permanent conquerors of the future. Contrarily, Mexicans are seen to live an endless romance with the past. Let us bring back to memory the central traces of Mexico, the changes it has undergone during the twentieth century.

Early in the century Mexico was a peasant country. Around 90 percent of the population lived in rural areas. Late in the twentieth century almost three out of four Mexicans are living in cities. Mexico is a basically Catholic country; around 90 percent of its inhabitants declare themselves so. But the fertility rate per couple has dropped during the past three decades from almost six children to approximately two. Demographic growth, which in the 1970s was above 3.5 percent, is now less than one-half that figure, 1.9 percent.

For more than half a century Mexico was ruled by a single political party. Today the opposition governs around 30 percent of the population. This dramatic change is also expressed in the public perception of fraud. One month before the elections of 1994, a particularly convulsive and difficult year, almost 75 percent of the population thought fraud would be committed. In less than five years and with intermediate elections ahead, less than 20 percent now hold that view. Economic change has received even more attention: the Mexican economy no longer depends on oil. Democratic institutions, weights and counterweights, have been systematically activated. Negotiations in the local congresses and in the federal congress attract the public's eyes, and the English term *accountability* is widely uttered among the opposition and members of the PRI, which already partially represents the opposition. Alternance in local governments is no longer a novelty. There remains the great unknown of what will happen during the elections of the year 2000. Almost 70 percent of the voters are characterized as the so-called volatile vote.

This is the setting of social demands to find common objectives for political parties, to find long-term objectives. A recent public opinion poll revealed that Mexican citizens are anxious to find a "new deal" that goes beyond competition among parties. The country's problems are still numerous. They range from the need to increase overall educational levels to being able to count on widespread administrative control mechanisms to subdue corruption. Today, however, the discussion about such issues is totally different from what it was only a decade ago. This book is a clear example and it sensitively points toward the discussion that is yet to come.

It is in this context that this publication can exert an important impact. Written in a simple style but with great seriousness—and with a large dose of common sense, which is always welcome—the book offers a global revision of the country. Many areas were examined: from natural and human resources, recent changes in the country's political life, the role of the church or churches, to contemporary

Mexican thought. The author's stern but respectful tone does not intend to turn materials into ammunition for one party or the other. The analysis is fortunately devoid of passion. The book is certainly not "neutral," however, because its contents are clearly aimed at examining the serious difficulties that restrain the country's full development.

Particularly rich are the presentations of different settings through which Mexico could traverse. They serve to show the huge margin for action that extends before Mexicans if we decide to make the future a field of consistent work stemming from our daily life. Beyond the polarizations and simplifications that have been so harmful for understanding the intricacy that is Mexico, and at the same time the complexity of the relationship between Mexico and the United States, this book can build bridges among Mexicans, as well as between Mexicans and the rest of the world.

FEDERICO REYES-HEROLES
Director, *Este Pais*

Introduction

> "Every few hundred years in Western history there occurs a sharp transformation. . . . Within a few short decades, society rearranges itself—its world view; its basic values; its social and political structure; its arts; its key institutions. Fifty years later, there is a new world."
>
> — Peter Drucker, *Post-Capitalist Society*[1]

MOST OF THE NATIONS AND PEOPLES IN THE WORLD TODAY are living through the kind of transformation Pete Drucker described in 1993. The shift from an age based on the industrial production of manufactured goods to one whose primary social good is knowledge is transfiguring the nature of human society the world over, generating profound new challenges as it opens up vistas of extraordinary possibility. Mexico is no exception to this trend, and this study traces how waves of global change are altering the landscape of this important nation.

At its core the fundamental transformation of our time is a shift from an industrial age to a knowledge era, when the creation, manipulation, application, and dissemination of knowledge, rather than the production of agricultural or manufactured goods, is society's defining activity. This new age holds immense promise to empower individuals, bring democracy to the home and workplace, and create a sustainable relationship with the environment.

But all major social transformations exact a price. The "major advances in civilization," wrote the philosopher Alfred North Whitehead, "are processes that all but wreck the societies in which they occur."[2] The rise of the industrial era, for example, caused immense social and economic distress, from the awful conditions faced by millions of factory workers to devastating social movements such as fascism and socialism. We tend to forget, when we consider the many problems that confront modern society, that we today are undergoing precisely such a transformation, this time to the knowledge era—

and that we should expect turbulent social dislocations in the bargain. Because of this larger context, there is now little question that the early twenty-first century will be a time of social upheaval, of reactions to the processes of globalization, democratization, and other aspects of our new age.

Such a major advance in civilization is under way in Mexico, and it is pulling Mexican society through wrenching changes. Mexican author and academic Jorge Castañeda noted in 1988 that in the last century the country "was transformed at dizzying speed from a rural, illiterate, backward, and largely peasant nation to the predominantly urban, literate, middle- and working-class society it is today."[3] Since Castañeda made that observation, the pace of change has only accelerated, propelling Mexico into the global economy and, increasingly, into the knowledge era. Along the way Mexico is evolving from a developing to an industrial economy, from a closed economy to an open one, from an authoritarian political system to a democratic one, and from a localized to a more global society. It is being modernized, globalized, democratized, and privatized all at the same time; and to make matters more complicated, it is doing all of this while straddling the fault line between two eras. In other words, Mexico faces the double challenge of achieving modernization and postmodernization.

Mexico is thus a country in transition—but in transition to what? This monograph offers a few ideas, but its central message is that the answer will be determined not by impersonal trends, but by the Mexican people themselves.

Mexico faces crucial choices over the next 5 to 10 years that will determine what kind of country it becomes in 20 or 50 years. In an important sense, Mexico is a work in progress. Trying to forecast in more specific terms where it will be a decade from now—economically, politically, socially, or almost any other way—makes little sense. What is of value is a better understanding of the tasks facing the country as it navigates the developments of the coming decade. Such is the purpose of this monograph: to chart the key trends confronting Mexico over the next 7 to 10 years and to identify what it will take to make this journey as rewarding as possible.

This work is the first country analysis of the Global Trends 2005 study, an interdisciplinary research project under way at the Center for Strategic and International Studies in Washington, D.C. After nearly three years of research into broad trends affecting the entire world—the results of which will be published as *Global Trends 2005: An Owner's Manual for the Next Decade*[4]—the project has entered its second phase of applying the general findings to particular areas of the world. To achieve this goal the country and regional studies employ several somewhat unusual analytical tools. "Issue Features" are short essays that offer an in-depth look at a subject or argument. "Surprise Scenarios" describe possible discontinuities—rapid, unexpected changes in direction that can occur over the next decade. Chapter 7, "Scenarios for Mexican Development," outlines five alternative paths that the country could take in the coming years. Its intention is not to make a specific forecast, but to propose a set of "indicators" or signs of the imminent emergence of each scenario. The foundation for these indicators is laid in the chapters dealing with individual trends. These scenarios are but one way in which the monograph seeks to help the reader make sense of, rather than predict, developments in Mexico over the next decade.

As in every Global Trends 2005 case study, a view of the challenges and opportunities faced by Mexico within the framework of global trends should further understanding of the country's prospects while also shedding light on issues of public policy in both Mexico and the United States. The general trends prompted the identification of five broad themes with overarching importance for Mexico's future:

- the emergence of a competitive democratic system;
- the importance of achieving a tempered, locally adapted form of capitalism;
- the dangers of extremist forecasts about Mexico's future;
- the importance of broad-based social investment; and
- the role of the United States.

Each of these themes is essential to the chapters that follow.

In the broadest sense, this study contends that the next decade will witness the full flowering of a new socioeconomic era. Virtually all social commentators agree that we live in an "information age," that the search for and use of knowledge represents the fundamental social activity of our time.

> Our favored term for this new age is "the knowledge era." It is a time when knowledge, rather than manufactured things, becomes the central economic good and the core organizing stuff of society.

Industrial-era society was primarily about *building* things—churning out vast numbers of tangible products. The knowledge era is about *manipulating information,* using it for its own value and to improve the efficiency of manufacturing. Neither activity excludes the other, of course—industrial-era businesses used plenty of information, and knowledge-era societies will continue to demand an unprecedented array of manufactured goods. No new social age completely replaces the one that had gone before; social transformations build on previous eras, changing them without abandoning them. But the overall emphasis, the focus of economic and social activity, *is* changing.

Taken together, the trends that make up the shift to a knowledge era carry dramatic implications for all aspects of human existence. They will rewrite the rules of economics, environmental policy, sociology, and political and military science. And they leave us with a profound sense of living amidst change. As Czech president Vaclav Havel put it,

> I think there are good reasons for suggesting that the modern era has ended. Today, many things indicate that we are going through a transitional period, when it seems that something is on the way out and something else is painfully being born. It is as if something were crumbling, decaying, and exhausting itself, while something else, still indistinct, were arising from the rubble.[5]

As Mexico moves into this new era, perhaps the most important single trend in Mexico today is the emergence of authentic multiparty democracy, replacing the one-party quasi dictatorship that controlled the country for most of this century. This trend's implications

Issue Feature:
Virtuous and Vicious Cycles in Mexico

One way of conceiving the daunting challenges confronting Mexico is in terms of a broad need to create **virtuous cycles** and avoid **vicious cycles**. The discussion of each trend suggests a key cycle or set of interactions that amounts to nothing more, or less, than bolstering the virtuous cycles and avoiding the bad ones.

- An example from chapter 1 is **demography and jobs**. With a million young people entering the workforce every year, Mexico can either foster a virtuous cycle of new jobs, a growing tax base, higher savings, and so forth, or suffer a vicious cycle of accelerating unemployment, poverty, inequity, and social instability.

- Chapter 2 emphasizes the relationship between **democracy and social reform**. The virtuous cycle encourages participation and accountability to solve social problems, while the vicious cycle stunts democracy and worsens social ills.

- Chapter 3 points to a connection between **reform and economic growth**. Here the virtuous cycle nurtures a more diversified and liberal economy, which spurs growth to create support for further reform. The vicious alternative is to rely on a handful of exporting companies, to ignore or encourage social inequity, and to retard growth.

- The subject of chapter 4, the interaction of **globalization and pluralism or tribalism**, can itself be either a virtuous cycle, with Mexico managing to combine the best elements of both, or a vicious cycle, with angry responses to globalization leading to xenophobia and protectionism.

- The relationship between **social authorities and social stability** is the subject of chapter 5. As a virtuous cycle this relationship strengthens new actors, such as local and state governments and socially concerned businesses, while indirectly helping to ameliorate crime and corruption. The alternative is a vicious cycle of instability and violence.

- Chapter 6 examines the intersection of **education and self-confidence**. Against a virtuous cycle of improved job skills and associated support for democracy and liberalization there is a vicious cycle of media-induced cynicism and fear of a future without adequate education.

range from competitive elections in the north to a more traditional, corporatist culture of political bosses in the south, with mixed forms in between. Still, the emergence of this long-term trend seems (at least for the moment) relatively clear, and expanding political participation is valuable not only in its own right but also for economic reform, environmental protection, and social equity. "Even if the lack of democracy is not Mexico's foremost problem," the Mexican writer and historian Enrique Krauze has argued, "the country's other problems cannot be resolved without democracy."[6] Or, as the late, revered Octavio Paz put it: "Only in an atmosphere of freedom and openness to criticism can the true problems of Mexico be defined and discussed."[7]

As elsewhere, democracy in Mexico is a double-edged sword. Growing popular involvement will complicate the process of dealing with social problems.

In the long run the necessity of political democracy for stability is obvious. It is an open question, however, whether in the short- and medium-term a democratic opening ameliorates or exacerbates Mexico's troubles. The answer will shape the country's fate over the next decade.

A second theme mirrors one of the most important conclusions of the general global trends study and is reemphasized in the final chapter: the reality of globalization and economic liberalization. These are hopeful trends, but the world's success at managing their side effects will be measured largely by its ability to channel them into socially beneficial avenues without relying on discredited statist methods. In the knowledge era this task is more important than ever—the pace of change is accelerating, the scope of globalization is unprecedented, and environmental risks are severe. For years Mexico has tried to move closer to industrialized-world status through privatization, trade, the favoring of business interests, and other conventional macroeconomic means. But if such measures are not better balanced by efforts to promote humane and sustainable progress, the country's social order could spin out of control.

This risk should not be exaggerated, and this case study does not paint Mexico as a nation on the brink of social collapse. But just as the last decade has witnessed the global victory of capitalism over socialism, the next decade will in turn show that capitalism, unfettered by social standards and norms, is destructive to humanity and its environment. The trouble is that the traditional responses to this fact—centrally planned government programs and mandates—have themselves often proved to be both inefficient and, in their own way, destructive of the human spirit (and often of the natural environment as well). How to bridge this gap— to reform and control capitalism without reverting to government paternalism—is a major social and political dilemma that Mexico, and the world, must address over the next decade.

Much of the recent literature on Mexico's prospects is filled with either dire forecasts of social collapse or rosy predictions of an emerging world-class economic powerhouse. History has repeatedly invalidated efforts to foretell the future and is likely to do so again, but extreme pronouncements about Mexico's flowering or doom still generate a good deal of interest. In exploring this third theme, the monograph opts for a less judgmental portrayal of the country, one with equal amounts of opportunity and peril. This is partly because a dizzying ride between confidence and despair has already damaged the modern Mexican psyche and partly because, although extreme opinions often dominate short- and long-term discussion, the medium-term outlook demands a more balanced portrait.

As with the outlook on general global trends, the broad prospect for Mexico over the next decade is neither optimistic nor pessimistic but a combination of intense challenges and opportunities.

A major implication of this fact is the country's own responsibility for taking advantage of its opportunities to progress. This in turn points to the fourth major theme of the study, the importance of broad-based investment in the future. A more secure and affluent future for Mexico will not happen of its own accord. It can only result from the right set of public policies, including investments in such areas as health, education, and a working legal system. The key achievement for Mexico over the next decade, making major strides toward becoming a stable, democratic country with a large and growing middle class, is inconceivable without such investments; but they in turn require the expenditure of enormous resources today by both outside investors and the government itself, and they must be directed wisely rather than by political convenience.

Surprise Scenario:
Economic Meltdown

By fall 1998, worldwide economic news had taken a decidedly depressing turn. The Asian financial crisis continued; Japan remained mired in recession and mulled the possibility of a major banking crisis; Russia's financial sector had very nearly disappeared; and the U.S. stock market had plummeted hundreds of points (although it later recovered). All of this had a major impact on Mexico's economy: By September 1998, the Mexican stock market was down more than 50 percent in dollar terms for the year and the peso had lost a quarter of its value.

This is not to suggest that these economic trends were set in stone. But the sudden tidal wave of economic crises highlighted a critical fact about the trends that follow: many of them assume, to a greater or lesser extent, continued economic growth.

This scenario thus considers the risk that Mexico's recovery from the 1995 peso crisis would be interrupted by a global recession. A long-term blow to Mexico's economic prospects would call into question its ability to meet the challenges spelled out below. At a minimum—

- **Social instability would rise** as millions of new job-seekers went without work, tens of thousands more lost their jobs, and anger, crime, corruption and anxiety mounted.

- **Mexico's fragile financial system could collapse** amid new waves of bankruptcies and declining foreign investment.

- **The tentative move toward democracy could even be interrupted** as the desire for political freedom took a back seat to the need for security and order.

Much thought over the next months and years will go into the question of whether Mexico is "headed for collapse" in an economic or any other sense. This monograph does not take a position on the issue—the goal is to sketch out long-term trends, not make short-term forecasts. But it is crucial to understand that any optimistic portrait of Mexico's future depends on a stronger domestic economy, growth of the rule of law, continued democratic transition, and other trends that would suffer at the hands of a protracted economic setback.

Finally, there is the role—sometimes constructive, often ambiguous, and more than occasionally counterproductive—of the United States. Centuries of contiguity have produced intense feelings of admiration and resentment on both sides of the border. Culturally, the two countries are blending in ever more fundamental (and to some, dismaying) ways. Economically, Mexico sends the vast bulk of its exports to the United States. The stance toward Mexico of the United States—and not just of Washington, but also of states such as Texas and California as well as of individual cities—will be just as important over the next decade as it has been over the last 200 years.

The coming decade will witness Mexico's collision with basic dimensions of the knowledge era, an era that is thoroughly participatory, decentralized, fast-moving, technological, tolerant, self-aware, and global. Although Mexico fully does not reflect those characteristics today, there are reasons to believe that it could—and could do so more thoroughly than many of the developing (or even industrial) countries that conventional wisdom has appointed as pacesetters for the new age. And there is, or ought to be, an urgency to these tasks: on a host of issues—creating jobs for new workers, easing inequity, developing new institutions to replace declining ones—Mexico is running a race against time. The race won't be over in the next 7 to 10 years, but by then it will be fairly obvious whether Mexico has made the right choices to win it.

Notes

1. Peter F. Drucker, *Post-Capitalist Society* (New York: HarperBusiness, 1993), 1.
2. Cited in *The National Interest*, no. 41 (Fall 1995), 18.
3. Robert A. Pastor and Jorge G. Castañeda, *Limits to Friendship: The United States and Mexico* (New York: Vintage Books, 1988), 14-15.
4. Michael J. Mazarr, *Global Trends 2005: An Owner's Manual for the Next Decade* (New York: St. Martin's Press/CSIS, forthcoming 1999).
5. Vaclav Havel, "The Need for Transcendence in the Postmodern World," *The Futurist*, July-August 1995, 46.
6. Enrique Krauze, *Mexico: Biography of Power*, trans. Hank Heifetz (New York: HarperCollins, 1997), 797.
7. Octavio Paz, *The Labyrinth of Solitude and Other Writings*, trans. Lysander Kemp, Yara Milos, and Rachel Phillips Belash (New York: Grove Press, 1985), 261.

1 ■
Trend One: The Foundations

THIS FIRST TREND BEGINS TO ILLUMINATE, on issues such as natural resources and the environment, the intense combination of challenges and opportunities embodied in Mexico's future. From advanced oil drilling technology to renewable energy to the empowering effects of knowledge-era business theory, the technologies and habits of the knowledge era could allow Mexico to achieve sustainable—and sustained—growth. Taking advantage of those opportunities, however, requires the right political decisions, and the evidence on whether Mexico is stepping up to this requirement remains mixed.

A number of demographic, natural resource, environmental, and cultural factors establish the context in which other trends unfold. During the next 10 years these factors should remain relatively constant—that is, prices should be more or less stable and no major global discontinuities should occur. Within this general stability, however, two overarching issues are paramount. One is a *growing urgency for long-range planning* to address needs that, although they will not mature in the next decade, nonetheless demand action during this period. The second is the risk that a combination of factors—smaller held reserves, shrinking gaps between supply and demand, the growing role of perception in setting prices—will conspire to produce a series of *recurrent and unpredictable price spikes* amid generally sufficient supply in major categories of natural resources.

A Story of Two Worlds

The first aspect of this trend involves two issues, *demography* and *the environment*, each of which reveals sharp distinctions between the industrial and developing worlds.

In terms of demography the global situation is simple: the developing world's population is growing fast, while the populations of the industrial world are stagnant and aging. Overall, additions to the world's population are occurring at a staggering rate. After spending almost two millennia producing its first 1 billion people, the human race added a second billion in just a century and its most recent billion in little more than a decade. The world is now accommodating a growth in population equal to a new Pittsburgh or Boston every two days, a new Mexico every year, and very nearly a new India every decade. And yet because of such global forces as modernization, education, and the expansion of women's rights, all of which tend to suppress fertility, the world's population growth rate is actually declining. World population growth is not out of control, and in the course of the next half-century it is expected to level off and perhaps even begin to decline to a level somewhere between 8 and 12 billion people.

From 1995 to 2005, world population will continue to grow at its highest annual rate in history, increasing by roughly 800 to 900 million people to reach a total of about 6.6 billion.[1] This means, first of all, that massive population growth will occur in the developing world. Ninety-five percent of population growth between 1990 and 1995 occurred in developing countries, and that percentage will inch higher in coming decades. The bulk of this growth will take place in the relatively few countries located in what is called "the arc of crisis," an area stretching from sub-Saharan Africa through North Africa and the Middle East into South Asia.

This trend will also inaugurate a period of rapid urbanization in the developing world. Fully 90 percent of growth in urban populations over the next decade will take place in developing nations—an event with explosive ramifications, including problems of waste, water supply, air pollution, and alienation.[2] Burgeoning populations in the developing world will intensify the focus on youth. By 2005 almost 60 developing countries, including two dozen states in sub-Saharan

Figure 1
World Population, 1950–2010
Total population, world fertility rate, and annual increments of population growth

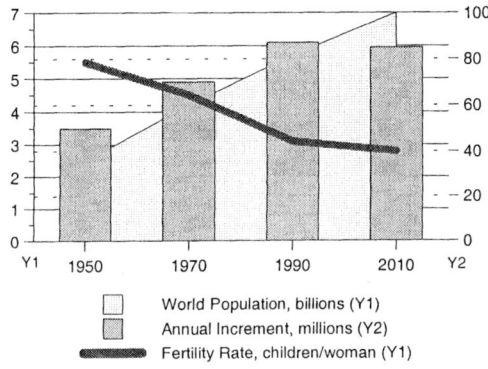

Source: United Nations, *World Economic and Social Survey*, various years.

Africa as well as important Middle Eastern states such as Egypt, Iran, and Iraq, will experience "youth bulges," with 20 percent or more of their populations in the 15- to 24-year-old age range.

If soaring populations have ominous implications for developing countries, slowing population growth in industrialized nations has equally disturbing implications. In brief, the industrial world is growing older.

Low birth rates and longer life spans, especially for the massive post–World War II population and the much smaller successor generations, mean that most industrial world populations are aging quickly: the number of people at retirement age (over 65 years) in industrial countries will rise 60 percent by the year 2025. The world's aging crisis is not unique to the developed world—many developing countries, notably China, face long-term aging trends as well—but it will hit the developed world first.

Similarly, in environmental issues there is a substantial difference in outlook between the industrial and developing worlds. In the industrial world, although total levels of pollution, greenhouse gas

Figure 2
World Grain Production, 1950–1990
Total and per capita on a scale where 1950=100

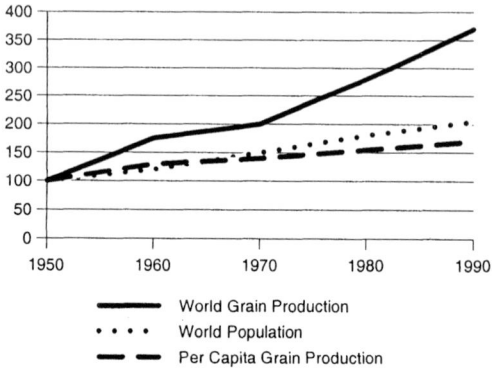

── World Grain Production
• • • • World Population
── ── Per Capita Grain Production

Source: Donella H. Meadows, Dennis L. Meadows, and Jorgen Randers, *Beyond the Limits* (Post Mills, Vt.: Chelsea Green, 1992).

emissions, and other forms of environmental damage continue to rise, pollution has been declining as a per-dollar-of-gross-national-product (GNP) ratio and often in per capita terms. This reflects an important trend: that a knowledge economy is better for the environment than an industrial-era economy, because it pollutes less and uses fewer resources. We are witnessing the birth of a radical transition to a social and industrial mode of production based on clean technology. Reflecting this new promise is the emerging field of industrial ecology, which focuses on reconciling economic growth and environmental health.

But this transition will be fully under way only toward the end of the next decade, and even then mostly in the developed world. In the meantime, pollution from the developing world is growing dramatically. Even by 1992 developing nations had overtaken the industrial world in terms of the levels of emission of carbon dioxide. Carbon emissions of developing nations are expanding three times faster than those of industrial nations. China alone, if its current growth continues, will emit more greenhouse gases by the year 2025 than the United States, Japan, and Canada combined.

A Price-Spike Economy

Just as they are environmentally more friendly than industrial economies, knowledge-era economies are also less dependent on natural resources. Creating knowledge demands fewer natural resources than does manufacturing goods. Nonetheless, population growth and economic growth will put new pressure on certain categories of resources in selected areas. Combined with "just-in-time" delivery techniques, the result may be recurring price spikes amid generally stable resource prices.

World food output, for example, has more than doubled in the last three decades. Food supplies per capita have grown by a quarter—a trend that has drawn in many areas of the developing world, where the quality of diets continues to improve. Moreover, the real cost of many food items has declined.[3] Globally, however, reasons for concern persist, and continued yield increases must be developed with further research. Even more alarming, a dramatic exception to the rule of ample food supplies will occur in the "arc of crisis" stretching from central Africa through parts of the Middle East and into South Asia, where exploding populations and continuing poverty will make food shortages a way of life, creating the need for intervention by numerous outside aid missions.

Growing worldwide population will also put new pressure on world water supplies. Eighty countries, mostly in the arc of crisis, already face life-threatening water shortages. By 2025 the amount of water available to those countries will have fallen by 80 percent.[4]

More people at a higher standard of living will mean greater use of energy. Once again, perhaps the most important part of this increase will not take place in the industrial world, where knowledge-era economies are more efficient in their use of energy, but in developing countries. In the United States, for example, energy use per dollar of GNP has declined almost 30 percent in the last 20 years. Still, energy prices should remain relatively stable through 2005, subject to periodic price spikes.

Oil prospects over the next decade involve a complex picture, with long-term worries and increased dependence on Middle East supplies intruding on a generally sanguine portrait of low prices and ready supply. The general baseline forecast has oil supplies rising

Figure 3
World Oil Prices, 1970–2010
In 1993 dollars

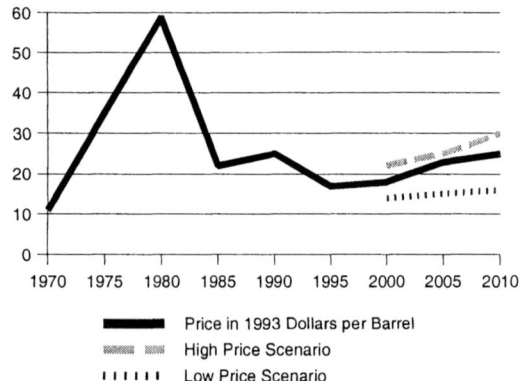

■ Price in 1993 Dollars per Barrel
▬ ▬ High Price Scenario
ɪ ɪ ɪ ɪ ɪ ɪ Low Price Scenario

Source: U.S. Department of Energy, *International Energy Outlook 1995* (Washington, D.C.: DOE, 1995).

gradually to meet demand and prices remaining under $30 a barrel through 2005. But to an extent possible in almost no other energy source, major surprises could be in store.

It may be too early, for example, to write off the threat of new oil shocks. Beyond the immediate dependencies of the next decade, the early twenty-first century could see an end to the world's "oil era." Peak production could occur sometime between 2000 and 2015 and begin to slope downward thereafter The exhaustion of known crude oil supplies will be accelerated by rapid economic growth in many developing countries, though some oil analysts believe that new discoveries and new usable sources of oil (such as oil shale) will keep the resource in more or less unlimited supply, at least for a half-century or more.

Finally, the next decade may well witness the beginning—the real beginning, after decades of fits and starts—of the age of renewable energy. Renewables will probably be the fastest growing energy source over the next decade. Such technological advances could, within a very short period, render more widely usable renewable energy sources (such as photovoltaic cells) cost-competitive with traditional energy sources.

The Foundation of Human Perception: Culture

A final foundation of trends in the next decade is culture, that amorphous combination of values, habits, religion, language, and other factors differentiating one group of people from another. In the simplest terms, the application of culture to the trends examined here involves appreciating the basic insight of sociology. As it was put by Peter Berger in his classic *Invitation to Sociology*, people are not "also" social beings but are "social in every aspect of [their] being that is open to empirical investigation. The structures of society become the structures of our own consciousness."[5] This basic connection between national culture and national character informs many of the national forecasts being pursued by this study. Clearly, some cultures are better equipped than others to succeed in the fast-paced, decentralized, flexible world of the knowledge era. Culture also has profound effects on relations among countries and other large groups or institutions.

Thus, in dozens of ways—socially, economically, politically, militarily—culture will exercise an important influence on world trends during the next decade. Developments that might otherwise tend one direction can be bent or skewed in another by cultural proclivities, practices, or preconceptions. But one thing cultural identity emphatically is not is a static, predictable, unchanging influence on the members of society. In fact, the engines of history outlined in chapter two are reshaping world cultures perhaps more profoundly and more rapidly than at any other time in history.

Applying the Trends to Mexico: Demography

Demographic trends may do more than any other single issue to shape Mexico's future over the next decade. These trends embody a daunting, but potentially promising, fact: in the next few years, Mexico's massive younger generation will start to come of working age. If these young people cannot find productive jobs, social instability and high unemployment could result. If, on the other hand, the Mexican economy can generate meaningful employment for them, it will inaugurate a new era of high growth, expanding savings and investment, and rising productivity—a virtuous economic cycle that

Figure 4
Mexico's Population, 1960-2040
In thousands

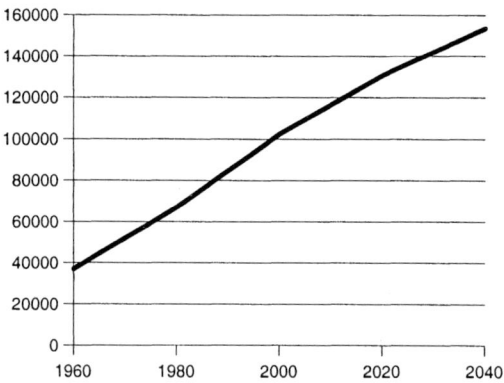

Source: United Nations, *World Population Prospects* (New York: UN, 1995).

will draw Mexico into the knowledge era as a solidly middle-class country.

Between 1990 and 1995, annual population growth in Mexico was only about 2 percent,[6] and the United Nations forecasts that Mexico's population growth rate will continue to slow, dropping to 1.78 percent between 1995 and 2000 and to 1.39 percent by 2010. This will bring the total fertility rate down to 2.37 by roughly 2005, meaning that Mexico, now adding more than 1.8 million people to its population annually, will be adding barely 1.5 million a year by 2010.[7] From a longer-term perspective, however, the country's population has grown rapidly: from about 50 million in 1970 to more than 93 million in 1995, 106 million in 2005, nearly 118 million by 2010, and 143 million in 2030. Within a single lifetime Mexico's population will have tripled.[8]

The result is that Mexico is both notably young and slowly growing older. In 1995, 57 percent of the population was 24 years old or younger, while 36 percent was 14 or younger. But because of its slowing birth rate, Mexico is aging: the percentage of the population age 60 or over will grow from 5.8 percent in 1990 to almost 8.5 percent by 2010, and Mexico's median age in the same period will rise from 20 to 27.[9] Eventually, in the fairly distant future, this will mean the

Figure 5
Mexico's Young But Aging Population, 1970–2010
Median age and percentage under 15

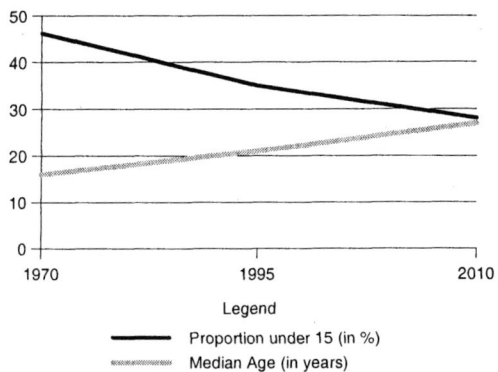

Legend
——— Proportion under 15 (in %)
▬▬▬ Median Age (in years)

Source: INEGI (<www.inegi.gob.mx>)

skyrocketing pension and health care burden typical of aging societies.

The most urgent economic issue tied to demography is employment. As the younger generations age, Mexico's workforce will grow by a third in 10 years, swelling from its present size of almost 36 million to nearly 50 million. The country must generate roughly a million jobs a year to provide employment for all the young people entering the workforce—and this from an economy whose number of officially registered workers increased by only that much between 1988 and 1995.[10] As Robert Kaplan has put it, to "create enough menial jobs, Mexico's economy must grow by six percent annually. To create good jobs and move the country into the First World the economy would have to grow by nine or 10 percent."[11]

Recent reports on job creation are mixed: in 1996, one important measure of permanent employment—the number of workers insured in the social security system—rose by just over 660,000, although a more recent estimate suggests that impressive recent growth will create twice that number of new jobs in 1998. And with much of the world seemingly headed into recession in late 1998, Mexico's growth prospects for the coming years looked suddenly worse; at the time,

Surprise Scenario:
A Massive Earthquake

A possible surprise for Mexico during the next decade is a massive earthquake, as large as or larger than the one that struck the country in 1985. As that event showed, natural disasters in Mexico (as elsewhere) are often more than fleeting acts of fate—they can carry immense political, social, and economic ramifications.

This time, the toll of a large earthquake in central Mexico, and especially in the capital, is potentially huge. Several thousand people perish, hundreds of thousands of others are left homeless, hundreds of businesses are destroyed, and Mexican government institutions are damaged physically as well as perceptually.

Unless the Mexican army is able to implement its sophisticated disaster relief plans with great success, the event will shake the Mexican political system to its foundations, figuratively as well as literally. Blame for the failure to deal effectively with the disaster can fall squarely on the country's fledgling democracy, thereby threatening to slam the democratic opening shut. Specific implications include the following:

- **Popular outcry and revulsion with politics as usual.** Much will hinge on the quality of the government response. Inefficient official relief, especially if it is revealed that corruption and favoritism play a role, will yet again undermine public confidence—but this time, in the democratic institutions.

- **Economic damage.** The country could fall into a new recession if the damage to businesses in and around Mexico City is sufficiently severe. Savings earmarked for investment may have to be redirected to reconstruction.

- **Changed relations with the United States.** The U.S. reaction to the disaster will no doubt be closely watched. Managed carefully, a helping hand will solidify ties; managed badly (or not at all), it could damage ties further.

- **A bolstered profile for the Mexican military.** If the army moves in forcefully while the politicians appear confused, it could assume a greater role in the country's society, politics, and economy—for good or ill.

some economists had downgraded estimates of the 1998 growth rate to about 4.5 percent, with an expectation of 2 percent or less in 1999.[12]

If job creation consistently lags behind demand in coming years, says Grupo Financiero Inverlat, "unemployment and underemployment will remain high, stressing the polarization of the Mexican society."[13] Failure to provide sufficient jobs also risks a massive new wave of illegal immigration to the United States, engendering new U.S.-Mexican tensions.

Yet the rush of young Mexicans to join the workforce also contains the potential for a very promising scenario.

If jobs can be found for the new workers, dependency ratios will decline substantially over the coming decades, freeing resources for social investment. For the first time in a century, workers will outnumber children, opening opportunities to fashion a sizable middle class out of the ballooning workforce. If it can provide sufficient good jobs for its young people, and if those young people can be persuaded to save significantly, Mexico could lay the groundwork for a more stable and prosperous future. As the country begins to make progress on jobs and savings, its dependency ratio will further decline. Achieving this virtuous cycle will be extremely difficult. For one thing, relatively few observers of the Mexican economy expect consistent economic growth in the range of 8 percent or more.

A large younger population also bodes well for Mexico's ability to meet the psychosocial demands of the knowledge era. As discussed in chapters 4 and 6, accelerating globalization and other changes intrigue younger people as much as they intimidate older ones. There is abundant evidence that many of the country's young people are eager for the opportunities and challenges of a global era.

Mexico also represents an important case study for one of the world's somewhat more ambiguous demographic phenomena: urbanization. Mexico is already 75 percent urban and Mexico City ranks as one of the world's largest megacities. The process of urbanization will continue (albeit somewhat more slowly) over the next decade. Intense urban concentrations cannot help but foster severe social tensions.[14] But the knowledge era and its new technologies (such as wireless communications and renewable energy) intensify as

Figure 6
Ultimately, An Old Population: Percentage of Population over 60, 1990–2075

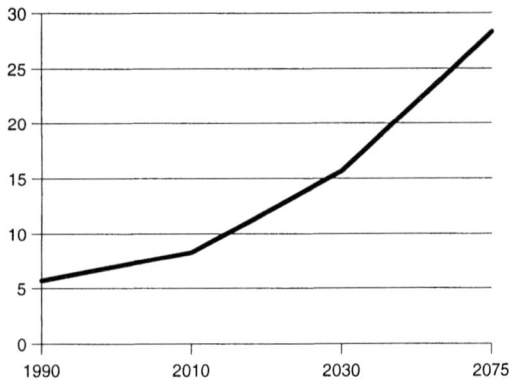

Source: World Bank, *Averting the Old Age Crisis* (Washington, D.C.: World Bank, 1994).

well the economic and social attractions of non-urban areas. The growth of Mexico City is already slowing; economic openness has forced many industries that once operated in the capital out of business, which combined with the lure of jobs in the north and a declining quality of life in the city's basin has reduced population growth. United Nations projections for Mexico City's population in 2000 have dropped by half since 1973, from 32 million to 16.4 million.[15]

The Environment

Mexico faces and will continue to face for many years a full-scale environmental crisis. The problems of the country's capital are well known: Mexico City suffers from some of the world's worst air quality, an urgent water problem, and other ecological emergencies. But a host of other environmental crises as severe as those in Mexico City threaten to turn much of the country into an ecological disaster area.

At the same time, Mexico is on the verge of major economic expansion at a time when sustainable development has taken on real meaning. For example, Mexico's transportation needs will multiply just as a number of automobile, truck, and passenger bus manufacturers are coming out with very low-emission (and even zero-emission) vehicles. Mexico's energy demands will surge as a number of leading renewable energy technologies become cost-competitive with fossil fuels. Thus even though the country may begin to pollute at unprecedented levels, its options for dealing with pollution will be more advanced than ever.

The potential exists for Mexico to become an example among developing countries of clean, sustainable development. But this cannot be achieved without hard work, visionary and sometimes controversial public policy, and, above all, the active interest and support of the Mexican people.

Mexico's actual environmental situation is far removed from this ideal. Aside from the country's water crisis—which is perhaps its most urgent ecological challenge, as discussed below—Mexico confronts a daunting array of interrelated environmental disasters.[16]

- Overfarming and excessive use of fertilizers have ruined much of the countryside. "Nearly a third of the country's 50 million acres (20 million hectares) of farmland have been severely eroded; 86 percent is suffering erosion of some degree." In the state of Oaxaca, 70 percent of once-arable land can no longer be farmed. Environmentalists forecast that without substantial recovery efforts the state of Tlaxcala could become a desert by 2010.

- Mexico has the highest rate of deforestation of any country in the world. Yet its rain forests are among the richest reservoirs of biological material.

- Pollution and chemical waste are widespread and the "intensive and uncontrolled use of pesticides" kills 5,000 people a year nationwide. In 1991 alone Mexico used 3 million tons of fertilizers and 2 million tons of insecticides.

- The border area, where companies do business free from the prying eyes of the U.S. Environmental Protection Agency, has become one of the most polluted areas in the hemisphere.[17] In one locality, government studies found that more than 16 percent of the population had skin disease and almost 10 percent had respiratory illness—not surprising, given that creek water near one set of factories had 3,400 times the amount of lead pollution and more than 1,200 times the cadmium allowed by U.S. law.

- Some agricultural fields outside the capital irrigate their crops with "black water," or wastewater, pumped from the city. Mexico City's water treatment plants can purify less than 10 percent of its wastewater,[18] and because Mexico City's sewage flows into several river headwaters, "even if you hike into a remote canyon downstream, you will have to wade through a river full of foam and chemicals." Pemex, the national oil company, remains a large polluter and has delayed its compliance with new environmental standards.

In sum, the damage to Mexico's ecology is "so severe that environmental destruction is threatening to undermine future growth."[19] Environmental degradation is, for example, tied to poverty: 85 percent of the country's 28,000 collective farms (*ejidos*) rely on agriculture for the livelihood of their people, yet only 12 percent of their land is arable.[20] When the land collapses, many people head for cities. Those who remain in the countryside—and although the percentage of rural Mexicans has dropped to 25 percent, absolute numbers on farms grew from 14 million in 1950 to 22.5 million in 1990—are desperately poor.

The centerpiece of the country's ecological catastrophe is Mexico City, where surrounding mountains and a thermal inversion keep pollution, dirt, fecal dust, and other particles trapped in the air. Mexico City's 3 million to 4 million cars burn 5 million gallons of gasoline a day, creating 8,000 tons of pollution—every day. Solar rays produce ozone from the chemicals in the air,[21] and ozone levels exceed safe levels just about every day of the year. "To live in Mexico City," Eugene Linden has written, "is to live in a place where the basic elements of life—air, water, and soil—have become inimical to health."[22]

Issue Feature:
Environmental Progress

Signs of a legitimate environmental protection program have emerged in Mexico, necessary first steps toward solutions.

- President Ernesto Zedillo consolidated cross-cutting environmental agencies into a single, cabinet-level secretariat, the Secretaría de Medio Ambiente, Recursos Naturales y Pesca, known as Semarnap. Its regulatory authority has been enhanced, as reflected in broad changes to the General Environmental Law and new regulations in a host of areas.

- New laws on labor and health that came into effect in 1997 mandate improved disposal and cleanup of toxic waste. This has created the potential for environmental remediation, a market that remains quite small in Mexico, to expand significantly.[23]

- A new National Water Commission program requires all 134 municipalities with populations exceeding 50,000, as well as 1,000 businesses that generate pollution outside those areas, to submit plans for meeting stringent new water cleanliness standards that go into force in the year 2000. Companies that comply—by, for example, investing in water treatment technology—will earn hefty tax benefits; those that fail to comply will face large fines. The program's goal is to sanitize 90 percent of all water emissions within 15 years.[24]

- The government has granted special trade status to certain categories of environmental technology, giving Mexican firms easier access to cutting-edge antipollution devices.[25] Partly as a result of these trade concessions and partly because, as domestic savings rates grow, more capital will be available for environmental investment projects, the U.S. Department of Commerce has identified Mexico as the top market for U.S. exporters of environmental goods. Mexico has taken steps to enhance the capital available for environmental programs in the short run, through both domestic financing and international loans.[26]

- Mexico City, Guadalajara, and Monterrey have programs aimed at substantially reducing smog by the year 2000. The capital's program calls for more than $13 billion in investments between 1995 and 2000. Nationally, hazardous waste treatment grew from 12 percent to 26 percent of the total waste effluents between 1994 and 1996.[27]

One statistic that encapsulates the urgency of the capital's environmental crisis: By 2005 Mexico City will run out of space for its garbage, which is produced at the rate of 12,000 tons a day.[28]

The social and psychological consequences of these stark numbers are both obvious and unpredictable. Residents of the capital face a lifelong environmental assault on their health. Illness from pollution is common. Mexico City's air pollution also has a financial price tag: one estimate of its cost—from lost days of work, health expenses, and the like—puts the amount at more than $1.1 billion annually.[29]

Clearly, a continuation of these environmental trends is unacceptable. But in all likelihood, continued deterioration at the present pace will not occur. An important element of the solution to the crisis is democratization: as popular participation grows, environmental activism is bound to rise. Already an embryonic green party has won a handful of seats in the legislature, and Mexico's democratic opening will allow the connection to be made between popular desire for environmental quality and government steps to achieve it. Action in this area (as the issue feature "Environmental Progress" recounts) is well under way.

Another important part of the solution is to encourage a shift to nonpolluting knowledge-era industries.[30] Here, too, environmental and economic requirements are in sync. Improving the competitiveness of Mexico's nonmanufacturing economy must be an unwavering priority for the next decade. Many of the service and information sectors targeted—from consulting to computer programming to medicine and law—are environmentally friendly.

> Most ambitiously, Mexico—coming of economic age at a time when cutting-edge technologies allow for a reconciliation of ecology and economy—could initiate a major national program to become, in effect, the poster child of sustainable development.

Many Mexicans still view the balance between environmental and economic progress as a zero-sum contest. One of the most important public education campaigns that a Mexican government could undertake is to convince people that in the knowledge era environmental protection and economic growth go hand in hand. This is the message of the burgeoning industrial ecology movement, and the existence of that movement suggests that Mexico could marshal sufficient backing from a variety of international organizations, universities, and companies to use existing environmental programs as a jumping-off point for a host of more elaborate ventures: tax breaks and other incentives to attract renewable energy companies to do business in Mexico; cooperation with automobile companies to develop low-cost, low-emission vehicles for Mexico's streets;[31] a package of national investments and international aid to implement state-of-the-art water treatment technologies, especially in Mexico City; a meeting of the country's major companies to discuss industrial ecology; and other steps.

Such a bold vision of sustainable development would lay down an important marker not only for Mexico's future, but for that of the world. One of the critical challenges of the next decade is to help fast-growing developing nations progress economically without destroying local or global habitats. Mexico could set an example by pursuing responsible environmental stewardship—not only of its own land, but of the world as a whole. Unfortunately, little evidence of such a bold vision of sustainable development has so far emerged.

Natural Resources

The fate of natural resources in Mexico is somewhat mixed. Local and regional water shortages promise to be a major problem over the next decade. The country's oil industry will continue high levels of production, but its efficiency will be hampered by restrictions on foreign investment, and its foreign exchange earnings will be undercut by sluggish oil prices.

Water

The poet Homero Aridjis, one of the leaders of Mexico's nascent environmental movement, worries that Mexico City, which owes its location to its access to fresh water, will "die for the lack of it."[32] He may be right: although this death will not occur in the next 10 years—some estimates have put the exhaustion of Mexico City's aquifer three decades away—decisions taken in this period will determine whether the water under Mexico's capital runs out or is replenished.

Figure 7
Water Supply and Demand in the Valley of Mexico, 1990–2025
Volume in cubic meters per second

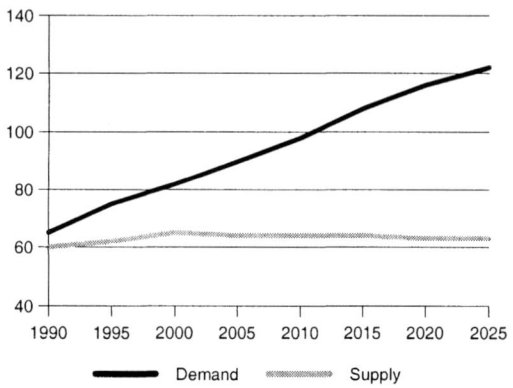

Source: Mexican National Water Commission (as reported in *Business Mexico,* May 1997).

[Mexico City's underground aquifer furnishes 70 percent of the city's water. Used at a rate of 63 cubic meters of water a second, the aquifer is being drained twice as fast as it is replenished by natural rainfall.[33] One result obvious to everyone who visits the city is that Mexico City is sinking into its mushy foundations; engineers have pumped so much water out of the aquifer that it is contracting, pulling the city down with it." After a century of slow subsidence," Joel Simon reports, "downtown Mexico City resembles a fun house at an amusement park. Streets are buckled; buildings are pitched forward or balanced at impossible angles." Mexico City, he writes, is now "thirty-four feet lower than it was when Cortés arrived."[34]

The gradual exhaustion of the city aquifer also imposes an ever larger financial burden on the government. Pumping fresh water out of the aquifer is increasingly difficult, and much of the capital's water is drawn from miles away. As a result, the water that emerges from the city's taps is unusually expensive. But it is not consumers who bear the price—every time someone flushes a toilet, takes a shower, or washes a car, the government pays up to 60 percent of the actual cost, with the price tag totaling as high as $1 billion annually.[35]

In the longer term, the ultimate risk is one almost unique among natural resource crises in the world: near-total depletion and a resulting social, economic, and environmental crisis. At its current rates of water use, Mexico City "will experience large-scale water shortages some time in the next 30 years."[36] Not only the capital but the country as a whole will feel the pinch in water supplies, because Mexico City will stretch the tentacles of its water pipelines further and further into outlying areas to quench its exploding thirst. Solutions to the water crisis—better conservation, repair work to capture the large percentage of water now lost through leaking pipes—are expensive and time-consuming, but they must be pushed forward if the country is to avoid a major catastrophe. In fact, several major water programs are already under way in Mexico City, but these projects must move quickly to avert disaster.[37]

Oil

Oil has played a decidedly ambiguous role in Mexico's recent history. Earnings from sales of oil on world markets have brought substantial wealth to the country, but inflated hopes about the scale and power of that wealth prompted disastrous levels of government spending and a borrowing binge in the early 1980s. The national oil company, Pemex, is a major source of government revenue and national pride, but its resistance to outside investment and privatization is creating an industry of aging equipment, outdated technology, and stagnant production levels.

Mexico remains an important oil producer—the world's fourth largest in 1995—and churns out more than 3 million barrels per day. There is, however, significant disagreement about the level of its total reserves, with the government estimating them at 69 billion barrels in 1996 but other sources suggesting that they are far smaller.[38] In a sign that Mexico's economy has matured, oil has declined substantially as an export commodity: the 1.7 million barrels that Mexico sends abroad daily account for 12 percent of its exports, down from almost 80 percent in the early 1980s. But revenues from the oil sector remain an essential share of the government's budget, accounting

Figure 8
Mexico's Projected Oil Production, 1930–2080
In thousands of barrels per day

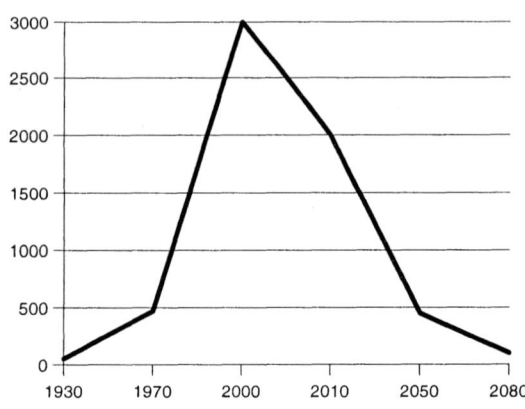

Source: C. J. Campbell, *Oil & Gas Journal Special Report,* December 29, 1997.

for almost 40 percent of all federal revenues. In 1996, for example, revenues from oil contributed more than 100 million pesos to federal government revenues of 255 million pesos.[39]

Continued low oil prices will hurt Mexico's export earnings. For example, although the majority of the country's exports are in a heavy-grade crude that fetches less than $10 per barrel, a 7 percent drop in crude prices (from $17.61 a barrel to $16.62) in 1996–1997 wiped out the advantage of an 8.3 percent increase in oil exports and even produced a slight decline in their overall value.[40] Government revenues take an even sharper hit from oil price declines, making less feasible precisely the kinds of social investment that are so crucial to Mexico's future. Both export earnings and government revenues are likely to embark on a harrowing roller-coaster ride of price spikes and temporary windfalls followed by a return to stagnant prices, a course that will be very difficult to manage. By September 1998, for example, Mexico had already cut government spending for the year by $4.3 billion because of falling oil revenue.[41]

Looking to the long term, it is safe to assume that Mexico's oil supplies will not last forever. Figure 8 summarizes one model of depletion; it suggests that, as for world production as a whole, the period 2005–2015 will be the high point of production in Mexico, after which it will gradually decline. To be sure, over the next decade oil will remain a dominant source of export earnings and government revenues. But the country nevertheless has strong incentives to begin preparing for a "post-oil economy"—a transition that is, in fact, already well under way in the export sector.

The Overall Energy Picture

The Mexican Energy Secretariat expects a growth of energy use at 9 percent a year through 2005,[42] rising by more than 11,000 megawatts from 1995 through 2004.[43] The country's total energy consumption is small by industrial world standards, but substantial in regional terms: in per capita oil equivalent tons, the United States weighs in at almost 8, Germany at more than 4, Japan at almost 4, and Mexico at 1.6—ahead of Chile (0.88), Brazil (0.66), and Peru (0.33).[44]

Official estimates suggest that electricity production must increase from 33,000 megawatts in 1995 to 54,000 megawatts by 2005.[45] Again, privatization is an issue: the state electricity company, the Comisión Federal de Electricidad (or CFE), continues to have a constitutionally protected iron grip on the transmission and distribution of electricity. The CFE cannot, however, afford the cost of the new power plants that will be needed, and it is inviting private companies to produce electricity to sell to it.

Here there is an opportunity for Mexico to begin a revolution in energy production by ensuring that a significant proportion of new energy comes from renewable sources.

This will be expensive, but the long-term dividends will be immense—particularly if the government can lure renewable energy production facilities to Mexican soil. It is hard to exaggerate the potential benefits of a growing renewable energy sector in Mexican industry. By providing jobs and drawing investment, it would place the country at the forefront of a nascent technological revolution.

Self-contained renewable energy facilities are ideal for generating power in remote locations far from existing energy networks, and this advantage would help combat urbanization in Mexico by boosting the competitiveness of rural and suburban areas. Cleaner energy production would help ease pollution in the short term (especially in Mexico City) while laying the foundations for long-term economic growth without peril to the environment. It is a goal to which every developing nation should aspire.

The Role of Culture

A final element of the foundations of global trends over the next decade is culture, in the broadest sense. Mexican culture is a powerful dimension of the country's national psyche and exercises an important influence on public policy.

In recent years, an emotional debate has arisen over the role of culture in inhibiting (or encouraging) worldwide development. A handful of scholars have amassed impressive anecdotal evidence about the importance to economic success of certain cultural values—thrift, creativity, industriousness, community ties. Some observers wonder whether the version of Latin American values that exists in Mexico may actually retard the country's progress.

One aspect of Latin culture that could hurt the country's long-term economic prospects is the emphasis on family loyalties to the exclusion of others. The top 70 firms in Mexico have, for example, changed little over time in their ownership structure and board membership: most continue to be dominated by a relatively small group of capitalists who are the offspring of several prominent families. There has been some change on the surface—new rich families rising to the top, a handful of firms changing hands—but on most boards the same families continue to wield control.

These are controversial claims, and not everyone agrees with them. In particular, it is important to distinguish between social norms that stem from a country's political system—such as the lack of trust characteristic of totalitarian systems—and more permanent cultural values. In other words, one must be very careful about definitions; the term "culture" has been tossed about with abandon in recent years, often without a clear idea of what precisely it means. It could be that what most see as "Mexican culture" is in fact a much broader set of political, social, economic, and cultural characteristics; that aspects of Mexican society resistant to the knowledge era are not cultural at all, but political or economic; and that the advent of this new era may burn off those barriers to progress, leaving a hard shell of resilient national culture—one entirely suitable to the knowledge era—intact.

A common complaint, for example, is that Mexican culture exhibits low levels of intersocial trust, in part because of the overwhelming emphasis on family loyalty. Octavio Paz has referred to the "suspicion and distrust" of Mexicans, which demonstrate "that we regard the world around us to be dangerous."[46] This fact would come as no surprise to the Coca-Cola Company, which found that "advertising campaigns emphasizing the concepts of reliability and trustworthiness did not work in Mexico."[47] And yet it could be argued that these low levels of trust are as much a product of the single-party state as of cultural values: one finds similar patterns in the post-communist countries of Central and Eastern Europe. If this is true, modest improvement in measures of trust should occur as political freedom expands—as indeed is precisely what has occurred. Between 1981 and 1990 the percentage of Mexicans agreeing with the proposition that "generally speaking, most people can be trusted" rose from under 20 percent to about 35 percent.[48] The key to consolidating social trust may be not to change the culture, but merely to build public institutions worthy of trust—a task examined in chapter 5.

The most important thing to understand about "Mexican culture" may therefore be this: Under the influence of economic modernization, economic and political globalization, and recent management theory, it is evolving in a manner that narrows differences with the United States and other industrial nations.

The experience of Mexico's northern states already provides strong evidence that "Mexican culture" can be perfectly hospitable to sound economic practices, provided there are sufficient incentives and resources. Even in rural areas there is evidence of attitude change, often prompted by the activities of returning villagers who had immigrated to the United States and then came home with substantial savings to start new businesses.

Perhaps the best discussion of cultural change in Mexico (and for that matter, throughout the world) is in the collected works of Ronald Inglehart, who has studied shifting norms and values in dozens of countries for more than 30 years. Along with Neil Nevitte and Miguel Basañez, Inglehart has carefully assessed the results of a series of surveys in the United States, Canada, and Mexico. Their basic conclusion is that differences in cultural values among the three countries are converging in a direction "consistent with the broad transformations that are taking place in most advanced industrial states."[49] The implications for Mexico include a less central role for the family, reduced respect for social authorities, growing "postmaterialist" values such as environmental protection, and increased political participation. These results do not in any sense imply the "death" of Mexican culture: the thesis of cultural convergence does not presume that modernization will wash away the landmarks of national culture in Mexico any more than it has in Japan or France or the United States. It does, however, suggest that Mexican culture will have to reform itself to accommodate the new era—a task for which, in many ways, the country is uniquely capable.

Notes

1. U.S. Department of State, *Population Trends Over the Coming Decade—Global Impacts* (Washington: U.S. Department of State, 1994), 1.

2. World Resources Institute, UN Environment Program, UN Development Program, and World Bank, *World Resources 1996–1997: A Guide to the Global Environment* (New York: Oxford University Press, 1996), 174–175.

3. See, for example, Donella H. Meadows, Dennis L. Meadows, and Jorgen Randers, *Beyond the Limits* (Post Mills, Vt.: Chelsea Green Publishing Company, 1992), 42–52; Paul E. Waggoner, "How Much Land Can Be Spared for Nature?" *Daedalus* 125, no. 3 (1996): 87; and Robert J. Samuelson, "A Coming Food Crisis? Unlikely," *Washington Post*, August 22, 1996, p. A31.

4. Robert Engelman and Pamela LeRoy, *Sustaining Water: Population and the Future of Renewable Water Supplies* (Washington, D.C.: Population Action International, 1993).

5. Peter L. Berger, *Invitation to Sociology: A Humanistic Perspective* (Garden City, N.J.: Anchor Books, 1963), 106, 121.
6. World Bank, *Trends in Developing Economies 1996* (Washington: World Bank, 1996), 340.
7. United Nations, *World Population Prospects*, rev. ed. (New York: United Nations, 1995), 736.
8. Ibid. The 106 million figure for 2005 comes from Office of the President, "National Population Program, 1995–2000," <www.presidencia.gob.mx>.
9. United Nations, *World Population Prospects*, 736.
10. Economist Intelligence Unit (EIU), *Mexico 1996–1997* (London: EIU, 1996), 16, 18.
11. Robert Kaplan, "History Moving North," *Atlantic*, February 1997, 21. The Economist Intelligence Unit, for one, does not expect such growth: it has projected medium-term growth in the range of 3 to 5 percent. If current growth rates continue, the most optimistic observers may have a point: 1997 growth exceeded expectations and has most recently been estimated at 6 percent. Economist Intelligence Unit, *Mexico: Third Quarter 1997* (London: EIU, 1997), 3, and Economist Intelligence Unit, *Mexico: Fourth Quarter 1997* (London: EIU, 1997), 18.
12. See Robert J. Samuelson, "The Crisis Is Global," *Washington Post*, September 2, 1998, p. A23, and John Ward Anderson, "Mexican President Addresses Nation's Ills," *Washington Post*, September 2, 1998, p. A26.
13. The 660,000 figure and the Inverlat quote are from Robert MacDonald, "Is Mexico Back?" *Business Mexico*, March 1997, 8. The 1998 estimate is from "Mexico Economy: Growth Shows Recovery from Devaluation," *Journal of Commerce*, December 23, 1997, on the Economist Intelligence Unit ViewsWire; the quote is from Ernesto Ceruvera of Grupo Economistas y Asociados.
14. From 1960 to 2020, land area per person in Mexico City will plummet from almost 3,000 square feet to 268 square feet. On average, by 2020 there will not even be land space the size of a small efficiency apartment for each person in the city. Mitchell F. Bloom, "The Next Generation: A World Forecast for the Year 2020," *Journal of Business Forecasting Methods and Systems*, 14, no. 2 (1995): 10–14.
15., Eugene Linden, "The Exploding Cities of the Developing World," *Foreign Affairs* 75, no. 1 (1996): 54.
16. These examples and quotations are drawn from Joel Simon, *Endangered Mexico: An Environment on the Edge* (San Francisco: Sierra Club Books, 1997), 36, 56, 74–75, 209, 211. See also Organization for

Economic Cooperation and Development (OECD), *Environmental Performance Review: Mexico* (Paris: OECD, 1998).

17. See, for example, Jeannie Ralston, "Among the Ruins of Matamoros," *Audubon* 95, no. 6 (1993): 86.

18. "Ecological Collapse and Poverty in Mexico City," *Swiss Review of World Affairs*, August 2, 1996.

19. Simon, *Endangered Mexico*, 246.

20. Ibid., 43.

21. Pete Hamill, "Where the Air Was Clear: Air Pollution in Mexico City, Mexico," *Audubon* 95, no. 1 (1993): 38; Exequiel Ezcurra and Marisa Mazari-Hiriart, "Are Mega Cities Viable? A Cautionary Tale from Mexico City," *Environment* 38, no. 1 (1996): 6; and Simon, *Endangered Mexico*, 78–79.

22. "Ecological Collapse and Poverty"; the quote is from Linden, "Exploding Cities," 57.

23. Jeff Wright, "Cleanup Time," *Business Mexico*, June 1997, 51.

24. Brian Feagans, "Water Watch," *Business Mexico*, May 1997, 49–51.

25. Jeff Jones, "Clean Break for Environmental Technology," *Business Mexico*, March 1997, 43–45.

26. Brian Feagans, "Green Lights," *Business Mexico*, September 1997, 38.

27. Ibid., 42.

28. Ibid.

29. Ezcurra and Mazari-Hiriart, "Are Mega Cities Viable?"

30. "The economic foundation of [Mexico City] must be transformed—with nonpolluting activities replacing the old industries." UN Environment Program and World Health Organization, "Air Pollution in the World's Megacities," *Environment* 36, no. 2 (1994): 4.

31. One report noted that the "ideal solution" for Mexico City's environmental morass would be "replacing the internal-combustion engine with some nonpolluting alternative." Hamill, "Where the Air Was Clear."

32. Quoted in Kaplan, "History Moving North," 31.

33. "Ecological Collapse and Poverty.

34. Simon, *Endangered Mexico*, 60–61.

35. Ibid., 86.

36. Ezcurra and Mazari-Hiriart, "Are Mega Cities Viable?"

37. One such program focuses on pollution and includes three wastewater treatment plants, a sewage collection system, and a water distribution network. Expected to cost $1 billion, it is to be financed with a combination of Mexican government money, funds from the Inter-American Development Bank, and a soft loan from Japan's Overseas

Economic Cooperation Fund. Feagans, "Green Lights," 39. See also Jeff Wright, "A Drop to Drink," *Business Mexico*, May 1997, 46–48.

38. See Economist Intelligence Unit, *Mexico 1996–1997*, 24; and Economist Intelligence Unit, *Mexico: Third Quarter 1997*, 25.

39. Economist Intelligence Unit, *Mexico 1996–1997*, 12.

40. Economist Intelligence Unit, *Mexico: Third Quarter 1997*, 25.

41. Anderson, "Mexican President."

42. George Baker, "Energetic Debate; Gas Tariff Limits Investment," *Business Mexico*, May 1997.

43. Mexican Ministry of Energy, "Major Advances in the Opening of the Mexican Energy Sector," <www.access.digex.net>.

44. Mexican Ministry of Energy, "Program for the Development and Restructuring of the Energy Sector, 1995–2000," <www.access.digex.net>.

45. Economist Intelligence Unit, *Mexico 1996–1997*, 25.

46. Octavio Paz, *The Labyrinth of Solitude and Other Writings*, trans. Lysander Kemp, Yara Milos, and Rachel Phillips Belash (New York: Grove Press, 1985), 30.

47. Andres Oppenheimer, *Bordering on Chaos: Guerrillas, Stockbrokers, Politicians, and Mexico's Road to Prosperity* (Boston: Little, Brown and Company, 1996), 269.

48. Ronald Inglehart, *Modernization and Postmodernization* (Princeton, N.J.: Princeton University Press, 1997), 306.

49. Ronald F. Inglehart, Neil Nevitte, and Miguel Basañez, *The North American Trajectory: Cultural, Economic, and Political Ties among the United States, Canada and Mexico* (New York: Aldine de Gruyter, 1996), 23.

2 ■
Trend Two: The Engines of History

THE FORCES LIKELY TO DRIVE GLOBAL TRANSITION during the next decade are the engines of history, propelled by science and technology as well as by social and psychological processes. These engines are sure to leave instability in their wake, largely in areas where governments and societies fail to anticipate the inexorable forces bearing down in their midst. Authoritarian governments (China, Cuba, Vietnam), closed markets and statist economies (Japan, Western Europe), and unreformed corporations face a precarious decade. Mexico, too, could find itself among those left behind if it fails to harness the forces of change.

The Engines: Science and Technology

Science and technology are perhaps the fundamental engines of knowledge-era history. Three areas of scientific advance are especially important: biotechnology, renewable energy, and information technology.

The announcement in February 1997 that scientists had successfully cloned an adult sheep in Scotland was just a marker on a path of unprecedented biotechnological research and discovery that is transforming the human environment. The Human Genome Project is scheduled to complete its map of the entire human genetic code before the year 2005. Such information, combined with the rapidly developing capability to manipulate human and animal genetic codes, will allow researchers to genetically identify the sources of illness and, eventually, to genetically engineer cures for them. U.S. companies are now seeking approval for some 300 biotech pharmaceuticals, some of which offer the hope of treatments or cures for such illnesses as Huntington's, Alzheimer's, and Parkinson's diseases, AIDS, multiple sclerosis, and various forms of cancer. Genetically engineered animals—the primary goal of the sheep-cloning experiment—will yield medicines such as insulin and even human replacement organs. The U.S. Department of Commerce estimates that "life patents" will be worth $60 billion by 2010. And biotechnology has applications in a still unimaginable number of fields, from agriculture to environmental cleanup.

The second area of technology on the rise during the coming decade is renewable energy. Its actual role in the world's power generation over the next decade will remain modest: the U.S. Department of Energy forecasts that renewables will make up just 14 percent of global non-oil energy production by the year 2010, or only 9 percent of the total energy sources. Although it may not witness the complete maturation of renewable energy, the next decade could easily set the stage for developments that make such a transition inevitable.[1] During that period, supplies of major fossil fuels should remain relatively plentiful, forestalling any major shift in favor of renewables. But this area of technology must be stressed for three reasons: first, its eventual emergence as the world's dominant energy source is nearly a foregone conclusion; second, the next decade will represent the beginning (but just the beginning) of this process; and third, renewables are now sufficiently close to being cost-competitive that a major breakthrough—such as a sudden technological leap to improve the efficiency of solar collectors—could set them at the forefront of worldwide energy policy.

The final and, in terms of economic and popular impact, dominant area of technological advance over the next decade is information technology.

In the next few years, massive supercomputers of unparalleled power will come into service. Other developments in information technology—miniaturization, better wireless communications, natural synergies between what are now different forms of information processing—will produce what can be called a "pervasive knowledge network." By the year 2005 if not well before, people will have access anytime and from anywhere to voice or video communications, the Internet or other networked computer systems, and an immense variety of entertainment options. Information channels that are now separate will merge, creating powerful and pervasive new information networks. This process will get a strong boost from new global satellite networks: in the next decade alone, 1,700 new communications satellites carrying television, wireless telephone, and Internet signals are scheduled to be launched, a quantity 10 times greater than the number of satellites now orbiting the earth.

The Engines: Social and Psychological Processes

The decade leading up to 2005 will also be propelled by a number of social and psychological forces that will continue to recast the character of governments and societies around the world. These include socioeconomic modernization, human needs, and social construction.

One driver of historical change that is a direct product of technological advance is socioeconomic modernization: the slow convergence of social and economic structures toward modern, technological, open societies. To remain prosperous and economically competitive, states must adopt similar forms of social and political organization—free markets and democratic governments. This process is homogenizing human societies around the world. But the process is hardly straightforward or predictable: progress always has its doubters and victims, and major social transformations tend to generate instability and alienation while fostering reactionary movements. The next decade will witness major counteractions to the cross-boundary, cross-cultural requirements for modernization and reform.

Another engine of historical change is human nature—the needs, desires, and aspirations of human beings. Classical theories of international relations or history have generally relied on simplistic formulas of human nature: we humans are either aggressive or peaceful, warlike or cooperative. A more sophisticated view of history, however, is available in the form of "human needs theory," which looks at how fundamental human needs—which might be boiled down to security, relationships, and identity—influence history in both positive and negative ways. In particular, the human need for identity or recognition and the instinct to seek security and a sense of belonging to groups have been behind some of history's greatest mischief.

Yet another engine of historical change is social construction. Human beings are social animals, and we exist within the contexts of our societies. The insight of social construction theory is that our understanding of ideas and events is shaped by social context. If we are raised in the United States, we are taught that free-thinking independence is a good thing and thus we are more likely to believe in it than if we are raised in China and are taught to think something different. The main lesson is that progress can build on itself: human beings and human institutions such as governments experience the world, draw conclusions from it, and modify their perceptions accordingly. In short, they learn. The speed with which this process takes place is strikingly manifest today in the European Union, a testimony to the lesson that peoples and governments have learned from a series of wars about the need for stronger shared norms and institutions.

Where Are They Taking Us?

In what direction are the engines of history pulling us in the decade ahead? They are pulling us toward three things: liberalization, democracy, and international interdependence.

One direction in which history will move, fueled by the energies described above, is away from state-planned economies toward free-market, open, liberalized systems. The last decade represented an immense step in this direction: the collapse of the Soviet Union and sweeping reforms in Latin America and elsewhere thrust more than 3 billion people into the world capitalist economy in just a handful of years. This process will continue, albeit at a slower pace, over the next decade. In some places this process involves the rejection of whole social systems; in others it entails a more gradual approach to reform by clearing away the barriers to development and competition erected by slow-moving, bureaucratic state structures. Yet despite the magnitude of forces pressing for it, homogenization will be achieved only at great cost: social and political discord, psychological stress, angry or anxious people expressing their cultural identity in

Figure 9
Economic Freedom in the World, 1975–1995
World average on scale in which 10 is perfect freedom

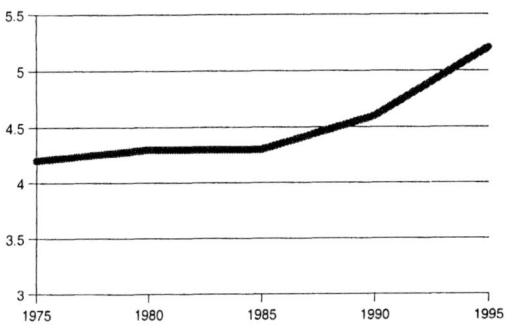

Source: James Gwartney, Robert Lawson, and Walter Block, *Economic Freedom of the World, 1975–1995* (Vancouver, B.C.: The Fraser Institute, 1996).

the face of onrushing globalism. These countervailing forces are likely to be so great that, along with socioeconomic inequities, "counterglobalism" will be one of the basic themes of the period.

The engines of history also tug the world further along the path of freedom and democracy. Expanded freedom is partly a product of economic liberalization: economic development and free markets generally produce free polities. But in his instant classic *The End of History and the Last Man*, Francis Fukuyama argues that a highly successful technological society need not be democratic. "The progressive unfolding of modern natural science," Fukuyama writes, "could just as well lead us to Max Weber's nightmare of a rational and bureaucratized tyranny, rather than to an open, creative, and liberal society." The mechanism of history, then, "needs to be extended." So Fukuyama draws on elements of human needs theory as first articulated by the German philosopher Georg Hegel. For Hegel, human beings seek above all "to be wanted by others or to be *recognized*." The human animal "was from the start a *social* being: his own sense of self-worth and identity is intimately connected with the value that other people place on him."[2] Thus in modern times the ultimate

Figure 10
The Advance of Democracy, 1800s-2005
Number of nations that are "free" or "partly free" and percentage of total states in those categories

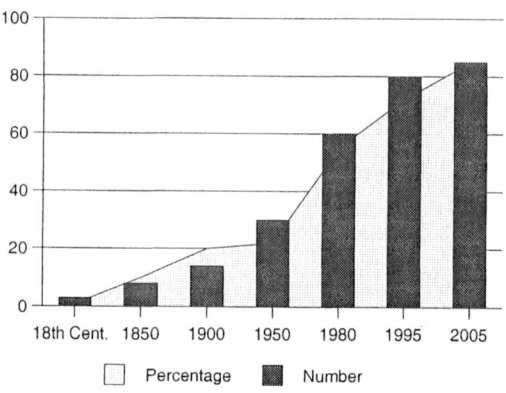

Sources: Freedom House and others.

source of recognition, the one political system that best allows individuals to seek recognition, is democracy.

Socioeconomic convergence also makes war among the converging powers less likely. In a world of free-market economies, free trade will generally prevail; and in a world of free trade, many of the things that nations desire—prosperity, goods, capital—can be acquired without resorting to force. The expansion of democracy tends to have the same result: by addressing peoples' needs for recognition without relying on external conquest, democracies tend to reduce the incentives for war. Empirical studies reinforce the principle that democracies seldom, if ever, fight wars with other democracies. More fundamentally, the human instinct to create reciprocal cooperative agreements to preserve security—the instinct that underlies the social contract within nations—can be extended to a lesser degree among them. Although hardly ending war or international violence, an emerging "global social contract" can create new mechanisms of harmony for dealing with violence in the coming decades.

Where Are They Taking Mexico?

There is no doubt that the engines of history have long collided in Mexico in spectacular—and sometimes disastrous—ways. As Enrique Krauze puts it, Mexico has been "a country in permanent tension between deep-seated tradition and inescapable modernity, between the devoted religious project of the sixteenth-century missionaries and the republican and liberal currents of the Western world."[3] Every historical transformation in Mexico has involved a struggle, every step forward a contest between the forces of tradition and those of change.

The difficult balance between past and future, the need to modernize and the desire to preserve a vibrant culture, make it imperative that Mexico tackle a task facing the entire world: moderating the impact of progress. Harnessing the engines of history is liberating and progressive, but hitching the entire country up to them involves risks and side-effects. Coming to grips with the underside of progress remains one of Mexico's overriding challenges over the next decade as it charges from one era into the next.

Inglehart, Nevitte, and Basañez contend that the fundamental historical directions outlined here—democracy, economic liberalization, and international interdependence and convergence—are real and on display in changing values around the world. But they emphasize that Mexico remains at an "earlier point on the trajectory," where this set of trends "has crystallized less sharply."[4] That is to say, history's course in the direction of freedom and global interdependence remains more tentative in Mexico. In the next decade the country could either assert its commitment to stay the course or make a stark U-turn.

Nowhere is this more apparent than in Mexico's still-incomplete transition to a fully open and competitive democracy.

Mexico's nascent democracy has sprouted from some distinctly antidemocratic roots. Even by the late twentieth century, the Peruvian writer Mario Vargas Llosa could famously refer to the Mexican system as the "perfect dictatorship"—authoritarian at its core, but embellished by ostensibly democratic and participatory institutions. This model continued through the Salinas years, when economic planners dominated the government and peremptorily forced their vision of national policy on the state.[5] But in the 1990s Mexico's era of democracy dawned in fairly decisive ways.

In July 1996 representatives of the four major political parties settled on a series of electoral reforms designed to promote free and fair elections. These reforms included campaign spending limits, electoral monitoring, and the direct election of the mayor of Mexico City. Elections in 1997 confirmed that these changes had made a real difference: the Institutional Revolutionary Party (PRI) lost its majority in Congress, the left-leaning Party of the Democratic Revolution's (PRD) Cuauhtémoc Cárdenas won the mayorship of Mexico City, and the right-wing National Action Party (PAN) increased its share of state governorships by two for a total of six. In congressional elections the PRI garnered 38.5 percent of the vote, the PAN almost 27 percent, and the PRD almost 26 percent.

The world values surveys analyzed by Inglehart, Nevitte, and Basañez also suggest that participation in Mexico's democratic process is growing rapidly. People have been empowered to participate in politics and society in unprecedented ways. Though increases in these categories are also evident in the United States and Canada, the authors contend that their growth "is truly remarkable in Mexico, which from a position far behind both of its northern neighbors in 1981, ranks almost as high" on various scales of political participation by 1990.[6]

In the medium and long term, the full blooming of democracy in Mexico is a hopeful and crucial trend. Democratic systems are indispensable for ensuring accountability, which one observer has argued is the only thing that "can begin to unravel the web of corruption and complicity that currently engulfs virtually every Mexican institution."[7] One of the new opposition-dominated Congress's first actions was to increase the period for consideration of legislative measures from 5 to 30 days, ensuring that government-proposed legislation receives a closer look. Popular opinion will be heard more readily on issues of interest to average Mexicans, and so democracy can contribute to resolving a number of major social ills that a closed and elitist political system left largely untouched—among them, corruption, environmental degradation, crime, and inequity. In the short run, however, politics is messy, and Mexico's evolving political scene

Figure 11
Political Participation in Mexico, 1981–1990

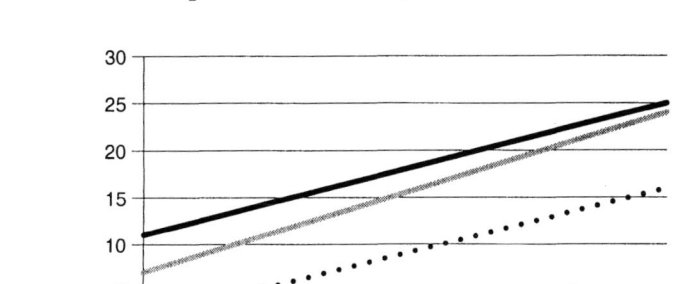

— % saying their political participation is high
— % who would join boycotts, strikes, or protests
•••• % who have done one of those things

Source: Ronald F. Inglehart, Neil Nevitte, and Miguel Basañez, *The North American Trajectory: Cultural, Economic, and Political Ties among the United States, Canada and Mexico* (New York: Aldine de Gruyter, 1996).

could impede decisive action on many of the country's key challenges—as it is already doing on such issues as bank reform.

As is natural at the outset of a democratic reform process, most Mexicans support the rapid expansion of freedom but have not begun to cultivate the institutions that will preserve their budding democracy. The coming decade must witness the start of such an effort.

The emergence of Mexican democracy represents something of a race against time. Can the country institutionalize its new parties and practices before they, like their counterparts in many industrial nations, are discredited amid a wave of public cynicism and mistrust (an especially valid worry in Mexico, where cynicism is routine)? There is the basic question—largely unasked in the midst of the flowering of free politics—of what democracy *means* for Mexico and Mexicans. Does it have the same meaning it has for Americans? What balance will Mexicans strike between freedom and responsibility, order and liberty, the state and the market? These are open questions and are already providing grist for the mill of political debate.

On a more encouraging note, an important aspect of political and personal empowerment spreading through Mexican society is gender and minority rights. Even as the country as a whole explores the limits of a newly opened political sphere, specific groups that have suffered discrimination will continue to do so in more focused ways. Indian groups are bound to heighten their demands for more equitable treatment and greater economic opportunity. An expanded women's movement also seems likely, in part to redress continuing inequity in policymaking circles. In 1983, of more than 1,200 members of the bureaucratic elite, only 65 were women. In 1989 there were even fewer, just 58, "most of whom were relegated to marginal positions (personal assistance) or 'ghettoized' in ministries such as education."[8] Mexican women enjoy more success in the business world, but democracy is bound to bring to the fore bitter tensions lurking under the surface of Mexican society, inaugurating new debates about the distribution of social wealth and power in this ethnically mixed nation.

Privatization and Economic Reform

The second direction in which the engines of history are running, economic liberalization, was evident in Mexico, as it was in countries such as China, before democracy. The creation of a more open, liberalized economy is well under way through such means as tariff reduction and free trade, privatization, reforms in government bureaucracy, and the fostering of the rule of law.

> The process of economic opening is bound to continue over the next decade. Determining the country's fortunes will be the seriousness with which the Mexican government takes on this job and the boldness with which it pushes the process into formerly closed sectors of the economy. But even the right choices will come at a price.

Economic liberalization has proceeded impressively since the 1980s. In perhaps the broadest measurement of liberalization, the

Figure 12
Mexico's Open Economy: Trade Liberalization Index, 1989–1996
Index of tariffs, non-tariff measures, etc.

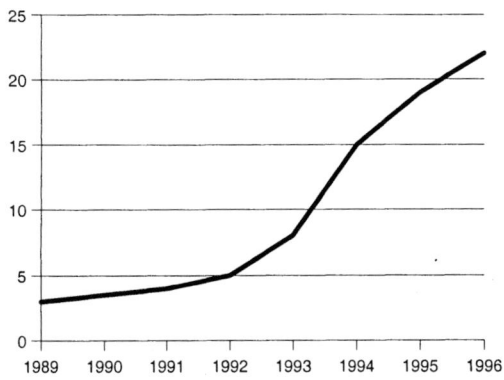

Source: Shahid Javed Burki and Gillermo E. Perry, *The Long March: A Reform Agenda for Latin America and the Caribbean in the Next Decade* (Washington, D.C.: World Bank, 1997).

---

total number of publicly held enterprises plummeted from more than 1,100 in 1982 to about 240 in 1991 and 185 in 1996.[9] During the term of President Zedillo, privatization has advanced in such areas as the social security system, maritime ports, railroads, warehouses, and natural gas and power generation rights.[10] Much more remains to be done in a number of areas. Among the most important areas for further reform is the financial sector: with many Mexican banks still struggling under the weight of enormous bad loans from the currency crisis, access to foreign capital often determines whether a Mexican company can make a critically needed new investment.[11]

The continued progress of liberalization will be sorely tested over the next decade in at least two ways. The first is the need to overcome major political hurdles to the privatization of two thus-far untouchable state companies: the Federal Electricity Commission and Pemex, the state oil company. Pemex needs help from outside investors, but full privatization of the symbolically important state company remains anathema to the authorities and Mexican governments have been forced to move slowly, attempting, for example, partial sales of petrochemical plants. Mexico pays a high price for Pemex's insularity: $1.4 billion in 1998 alone to import a quarter of all gasoline used by Mexicans (because Pemex cannot produce enough to meet domestic needs) and substantial international debt (according to one Pemex official, the company will need to borrow up to $7 billion through the turn of the century to pay roughly one-third of the cost of planned modernization).[12] The country's power-generating corporation could also benefit from worldwide participation and private-sector management.

The second major precondition for the vitality and success of liberalization is the rule of law: the establishment of the legal procedures and guarantees necessary to ensure the workings of an advanced liberal economy.[13] "Indeed," the *Economist* has noted, rule-of-law provisions "go much further than capital stock, natural resources, education, or the other usual suspects of textbook economics, toward explaining why a worker's productivity rises so astonishingly when he merely crosses the political boundary between Mexico and the United States."[14] Mexico has an especially long way to go on issues such as debt collection, land registries, transparency in transactions, intellectual property rights, and shareholder rights.

In all of this the political burden weighs very heavily. A number of privatizations, including in petrochemicals and the toll road system, have been scaled down or reversed in part because of political opposition. One observer writes that a handful of such failures combined with general economic hardship "resulted in what some economists term 'reform fatigue'—leading to widespread public anti-privatization sentiment that helped galvanize the [PRD's] political ascendancy" in the July 1997 elections.[15] The skill with which Mexico deals with such reactions to change will help determine how well it directs the engines of history.

A Regional Social Contract

The same forces propelling the gradual rise of a global social contract are spurring regional versions of the same phenomenon, often at a more rapid pace. In the European Union, Latin America's Mercosur, or the ASEAN grouping (Association of Southeast Asian Nations), we see blocs of contiguous states joining together to develop common rules and norms. The same process, impelled by the North American Free Trade Agreement (NAFTA), is under way in the Americas, where it will continue over the coming decade.

Inglehart, Nevitte, and Basañez have found important evidence that citizens of the three NAFTA nations—Canada, the United States, and Mexico—expect and support growing levels of political and economic integration of their countries. "Global change has eroded the importance of national borders," they write, and popular appreciation of this fact is growing. Astonishingly, a quarter of all Mexicans and Canadians queried in the world values survey favored abolishing borders between their countries and the United States, while nearly half of all Americans expressed support for doing away with the U.S.-Canada border. The authors' conclusion is that "political integration is *not* an unthinkable prospect for most North Americans."[16]

It would be wrong to exaggerate the importance of a few survey questions, and the authors may be stretching the implications of their data when they equate abolishing borders with "political integration." Nonetheless, the broad trend represented by these findings—less reflexive nationalism and a greater appreciation of the value of international norms and regulations—points in the direction of increased regional governance in the years ahead. The scope of many regional problems, from environmental degradation to drug smuggling and immigration, demands multinational solutions, and this fact, combined with the means for joint action established by NAFTA, will draw Mexico, the United States, and Canada into ever closer collaboration and union.

"The history of Mexico and Latin America," Carlos Fuentes has written,

> is that of a deep cleavage between a vigorous continuous culture and a fragmented, failed, weak political and economic life. To breathe the culture's vigor into political and economic institutions would be the primary answer to our present-day dilemmas.[17]

This trend in effect represents an extended proof of Fuentes's contention: further liberalization of politics and economics is inevitable—

and indispensable to the country's progress. But both transitions carry heavy short-term costs, and there is no guarantee that Mexico can weather them without major social dislocations.

Notes

1. See U.S. Department of Energy, *International Energy Outlook 1995* (Washington, D.C.: U.S. Department of Energy, 1995); William Hoagland, "Solar Energy," *Scientific American*, September 1995, 170–173; and Robert Righter, *Wind Energy in America: A History* (Norman: University of Oklahoma Press, 1996), chap. 12.

2. Francis Fukuyama, *The End of History and the Last Man* (New York: Free Press, 1992), 202, 206–207.

3. Enrique Krauze, *Mexico: Biography of Power*, trans. Hank Heifetz (New York: HarperCollins, 1997), 118.

4. Ronald F. Inglehart, Neil Nevitte, and Miguel Basañez, *The North American Trajectory: Cultural, Economic, and Political Ties among the United States, Canada and Mexico* (New York: Aldine de Gruyter, 1996), 55.

5. Miguel Angel Centeno, *Democracy within Reason: Technocratic Revolution in Mexico*, 2d ed. (University Park, Pa.: Penn State Press, 1997), 4.

6. Inglehart, Nevitte, and Basañez, *North American Trajectory*, 100.

7. Andrew Reding, "Facing Political Reality," *Washington Quarterly* 20, no. 4 (Autumn 1997):104.

8. Centeno, *Democracy within Reason*, 115.

9. Bank of Mexico, *The Mexican Economy 1997* (Mexico City: Bank of Mexico, 1997), 179.

10. Jeff Wright, "For Sale: For Better or for Worse," *Business Mexico*, October 1997, 8.

11. Shahid Javed Burki and Guillermo E. Perry, *The Long March: A Reform Agenda for Latin America and the Caribbean in the Next Decade* (Washington, D.C.: World Bank, 1997), 72.

12. Geri Smith, "Why Pemex Is in a Pinch," *Business Week,* July 6, 1998, 54.

13. See, for example, the analysis in Burki and Perry, *The Long March*, 12, 65, 75–76.

14. "Obituary: Mancur Olson," *Economist,* March 7, 1998, 91.

15. Wright, "For Sale," 8.

16. Inglehart, Nevitte, and Basañez, *North American Trajectory,* 136, 139.

17. Carlos Fuentes, *A New Time for Mexico* (Berkeley: University of California Press, 1996), 207.

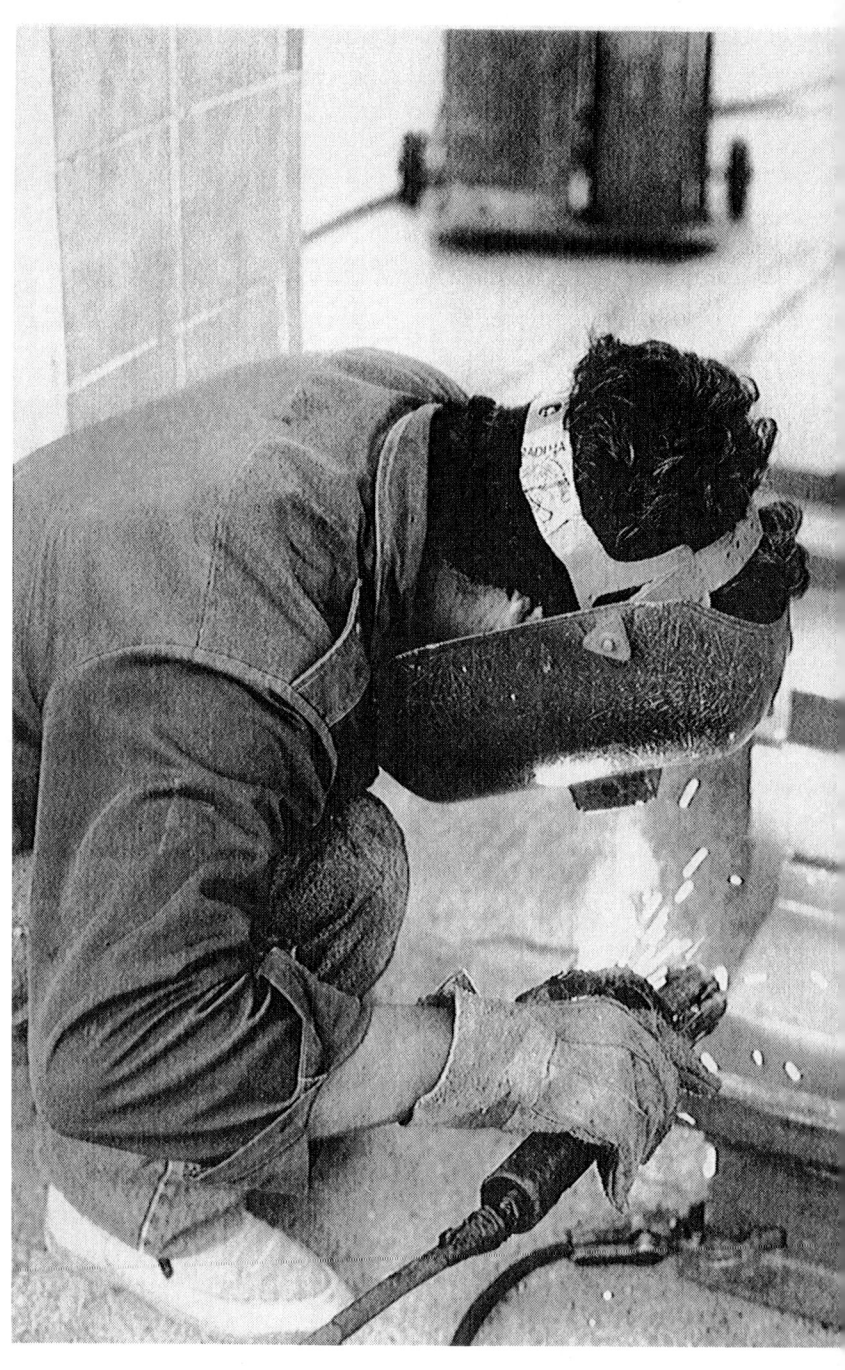

3 ■
Trend Three: A Human Resources Economy

THE STUNNING ADVANCES OF THE TWENTIETH CENTURY are changing the character of economic activity, even the very nature of what we know as an "economy." The essential trend is toward an economy based on intellectual activity rather than on agriculture, manufacturing, or non-information-based service activities. "Economic progress," notes former Citibank president Walter Wriston, "is now largely a process of increasing the relative contribution of knowledge in the creation of wealth."[1] Most of the new economy's workers deal in knowledge—that is, discovering, applying, and distributing it in such fields as computers, telecommunications, science, education, entertainment, publishing, health, finance, social services, and law. Because knowledge ultimately derives from people, this new economy is rooted in the rich soil of human resources.

Not all countries are marching in this direction at the same pace, of course. Mexico's task over the coming decade is as much to achieve industrialization as to transcend it. Yet developing nations that hope to prosper from their integration into the world economy will need to meet its standards and play by its rules. Mexico is no exception.

Two well-understood implications of a human resource economy are its declining use (in terms of per-capita or per-dollar-of-gross domestic product [GDP]) of raw materials and its bias toward the service sector. The U.S. Bureau of Labor expects 23 million of the 24.6 million new jobs created between 1990 and 2005 to be in the

Figure 13
World Trade in Services, 1980–1993

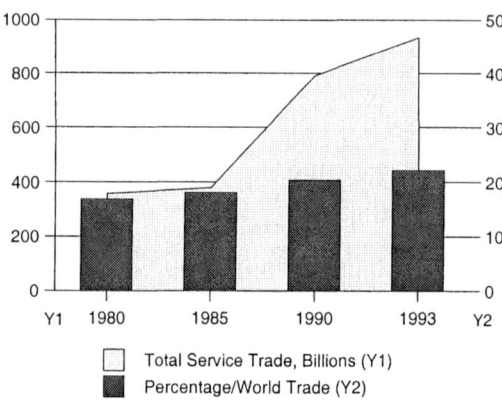

□ Total Service Trade, Billions (Y1)
■ Percentage/World Trade (Y2)

Source: World Bank, *World Development Report 1995* (Washington, D.C.: World Bank, 1995).

---

service sector. But, more than that, the knowledge era is producing more comprehensive, networked entities that might be termed "elaborated services"—companies that service a whole spectrum of integrated needs. A good example is an auto company that is involved in financing, travel, repair, fuel, and other activities related to car ownership.

As one would expect, an international economy based more on knowledge than on goods has witnessed rapid growth in the relative importance of service trade and foreign investment (figure 13). Economic statistics already reflect this trend despite the fact that existing means of gathering statistics tend to underestimate the true scope of service trade. Examples of services that are increasingly traded globally include software programming, back-office services, product design, research and development, and customer service. If outsourcing is a growing trend for businesses, it is taking on an essentially international character.

Elements of the Human Resources Economy

A more fundamental implication of the human resources economy is a transformation of the nature of work. This is a change that will affect every aspect of business and labor, from the organization of corporations to the character of the workplace.

An especially important institutional structure in the knowledge era is that of "virtual" organizations. These are organizations that exist only on paper—employees who work independently and communicate by electronic mail, telephone, and facsimile but do not always (or ever) share the same work space. Fewer organizations today are defined by their physical work space; many are composed of groups of people performing functions for which contiguous offices may be irrelevant. The key factor driving this process is the way the elements of the knowledge economy work together. Information technology encourages companies to automate and do their business online, for example, which in the interest of efficiency entails a reduction in the number of core offices and personnel groups.

Virtual corporations may also shatter the traditional distinction between big and small companies: smaller corporations can work together and marshal their forces to act as if they were one institution. Yet even as they create new opportunities, virtual organizations also have important—and vexing—implications for the concepts of trust and responsibility. How will businesses trust employees they rarely see? Not all cultures can adapt equally well to a virtual world, particularly those accustomed to hierarchical social structures.

The nature of business competition will also change in the new era. When corporations are fragmented among dozens of smaller subentities, bits and pieces of competing virtual companies can cooperate on specific projects. A world of virtual or networked corporations is a world of alliance projects, and the behavior and strategies of the businesses involved will differ dramatically from the more individualistic modes of competition in the industrial era. Cooperation will become second nature—interdependence will demand it, in the sense of cooperative alliances vying for shares in increasingly competitive markets. This trend underlies the prevalence today of cooperative, often disruptive new alliances in all industries, from partnerships between hotel and restaurant chains to ventures between traditional competitors such as Apple and Microsoft.

The principles of the knowledge era—principles such as speed, flexibility, decentralization, and empowerment—will change the nature of the workplace in fundamental ways.

The rapidly changing nature of employment has already produced frequent turnover and career shifts, which demand greater flexibility on the part of workers. Multiple career paths, serial careers, and less loyalty on both sides of the employer-employee relationship are now the norm. Employees' affiliation with their employers is more tenuous in such a situation, and the forms that work takes—until recently, a relatively well-defined 40-hour, five-day week—have become less stable and uniform. In 1993 more than 34 million Americans, or more than 25 percent of the workforce, were working part-time or as contractors.[2] These new and more flexible forms of work require a new kind of worker: better educated, more accustomed to rapid change, more willing and able to take responsibility for running important elements of the company.

A Networked Economy

Another development in the knowledge era is the growing dominance of networked organizational forms. No longer can we think of an economy as a fragmented collection of individual companies and people going about their independent projects. As virtual companies seek out partners for cooperative ventures, as information highways and superhighways bind together various economic activities, as finance becomes truly global, the appropriate metaphor for the new economic arrangement is the network.

James Moore's recent book *The Death of Competition* draws these themes together in a compelling vision of the future. Moore's basic argument is that businesses are not independent players competing against other equally independent industries, but actors interacting with competitors and allies alike according to a complex script—in other words, comprehensively networked entities. The issue is not that "competition is vanishing," he says. "In fact it is intensifying. But competition as most of us have routinely thought of it is dead."

The "traditional way to think about competition is in terms of offers and markets. Your product or service goes up against that of your competitor, and one wins." But this model "ignores the context—the environment—within which the business lies, and it ignores the need for coevolution with others in that environment, a process that involves cooperation as well as conflict." What we are witnessing today is "the end of industry," or the end of a time in which businesspeople can think of their industries as unique, separate things. The trick in the new economy is to break out of industry boundaries and "hasten the coming together of disparate business elements into new economic wholes."[3]

Finance and Capital

Inasmuch as money is essentially an information product, or a form of information, it should come as no surprise that finance and capital markets have attained unprecedented importance in the human resources economy. Even the stark numbers in this area—perhaps in excess of $2 trillion in foreign exchange is traded every day in the world currency markets, up from $10 or $20 billion in the early 1980s, while another one-quarter trillion dollars is traded daily in bond and equity transactions—do not do justice to the critical role of finance in the new economy.

For one thing, finance serves as an enforcer and ratifier of socio-economic convergence. Only countries that reform and liberalize attract the investment they need to remain prosperous and maintain growth. *New York Times* columnist Thomas Friedman calls this coercive pressure "the paradigm," an international model of social and economic organization demanded by capital markets. While the long-term effects of democracy and economic liberalization are generally positive, heavy short-term costs are paid by nations dragged into such transitions more quickly and more deeply than they had expected.

But perhaps the most important trend in this area is the fact that finance itself is in the midst of a revolution, one involving the elimination of middlemen (such as stockbrokers) and the new ability of individuals to manage their own financial affairs online, a process accelerating the emergence of "e-cash." Within 10 years we may no longer think of money as a tangible object; it may exist only in cyberspace, shuffled rapidly between bank accounts, mutual funds, insurance funds, loans, and dozens of other applications. We are to some extent entering a world of "virtual economics," in which the strength of an economy will be judged in perceptual as much as in real terms. It may turn out that virtual economies are more prone to sudden peaks and valleys, and more susceptible to boom-and-bust cycles, than industrial-era economies.

Worsening Income Distribution

A globalized human resource economy threatens to stretch the gap between haves and have-nots in both industrial and developing countries. Several factors are responsible: new distinctions in income between high-paying, high-tech jobs and low-paying service jobs; social divisions fostered by the demand for highly educated workers in many new positions; the stratifying effects of a global economy that imposes global wage standards on industrial economies; and stark divisions created by the rise of alternatives to full-time employment, including temporary and part-time jobs.

Evidence supporting this development is widespread, at least in the United States. In the 1980s an astounding 62 percent of new national wealth went to the top 1 percent of the population, while 37 percent went to the next 19 percent and a paltry 1 percent to the remaining 80 percent of Americans. Worldwide the story is much the same: between 1960 and 1990, the incomes of the richest 20 percent grew three times faster than those of the poorest 20 percent. In 1960 the richest fifth held three-quarters of the world's income and the poorest fifth just 2.3 percent. By 1990 the richest fifth held 85 percent of global income and the poorest fifth an astonishingly meager 1.4 percent.[4]

An especially disturbing pattern is the immense disparity in college degrees acquired by children of wealthy and middle-class families in the United States. Families with incomes of $67,000 or greater see 80 percent of their children attend and graduate from college. The corresponding figure for families with incomes between $20,000 and $67,000 is just 20 percent, and for poorer families, less than 10 percent.[5] This situation cannot persist if America is to retain its egalitarian nature in a knowledge era.

Figure 14
The Rise of the Developing World
Developing nations' share of world output in regular and purchasing-power parity measures, 1970–2010

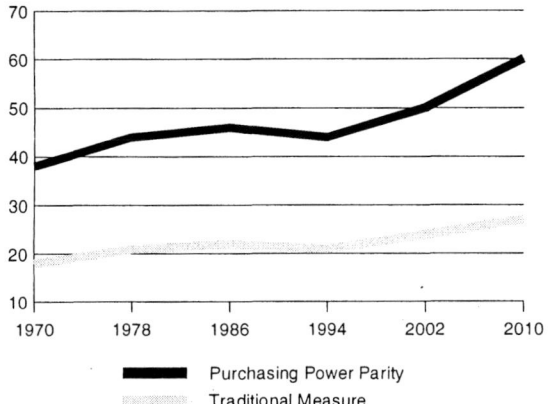

Source: World Bank, *Global Economic Prospects and the Developing Countries* (Washington, D.C.: World Bank, 1995).

Clearly, in an age that emphasizes specialized knowledge, education, and high-technology skills, a new social and economic wedge might emerge between the knowledge-proficient and the knowledge-deprived. At the same time, with the ascendancy of market-based solutions and the accompanying decline in governmental authority, knowledge-era societies may find it more difficult to effectively solve the problem of socioeconomic inequity.

Shift to the Developing World

The broad trends considered here will also promote a relative shift of power, especially economic power, to the developing world, with the new locus in the emerging markets in Asia. A basic reason for this change has been the difference in economic growth rates: only 2 percent in the industrial countries, compared to 4–7 percent in many parts of the developing world, through the late 1990s.

This transfer of power represents a tectonic shift in the foundations of world politics. Power is being redistributed from industrial nations to developing ones, making the world community more multipolar in the process. This will not happen overnight; some developing nations, such as China, will still have per capita incomes under $1,000 by 2005. According to even traditional measures, however—rather than the "purchasing power parity" measures that inflate their economic importance—the clout of developing nations is growing. By the year 2010, these nations will account for 30 percent of world imports and 22 percent of exports (up from 24 and 17 percent today). As the World Bank concludes, the rise of the developing world means that "by 2010 more than one billion consumers in developing countries could have per capita incomes exceeding those of Greece or Spain today."[6] Within a decade or so, U.S. exports to emerging market countries will outpace exports to Europe and Japan combined. Successful knowledge-era companies will find ways to reach this immense new market with goods and services.

The Trends and Mexico: The Decisive Role of Economics

If demographics are the most important single force shaping Mexico's medium-term future, it is in economics that we find the indispensable foundation for achieving all other social and political goals. Mexico's economy is still far from the virtual, networked, high-technology future, and only strong and well-directed growth can close this gap.

> With vigorous economic growth, lively job creation, rising productivity, and accelerated national savings and investment, Mexico can begin to meet its social and political challenges in the next decade. But in the absence of strong economic performance, there is no guarantee that the country can make it through the next 10 years without grave instability.

This is particularly true because economics is so important to the Mexican people. In a 1994 poll that asked respondents to rank the "most important issues facing the country," almost 40 percent answered either unemployment or "economic problems." The next highest-ranked answers were "social problems" (which include inequity and other economic issues) and "poverty," which together totaled more than 18 percent. The first completely noneconomic issue to

Figure 15
Mexico's Exports, 1995
In millions of dollars

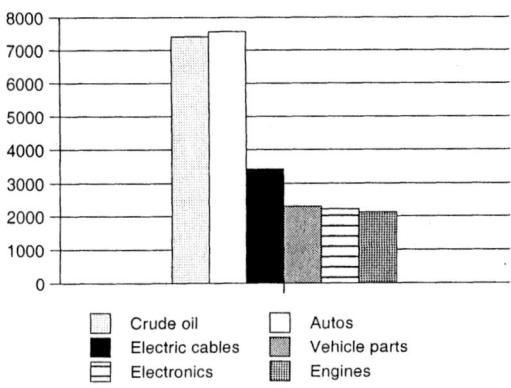

Source: Economist Intelligence Unit, *Mexico Country Profiles 1996–1997* (London: EIU, 1996).

make the list was corruption, in fifth place with 7.6 percent. Lack of democracy came in ninth, with merely 3.4 percent of respondents nominating it as the most important issue facing Mexico in the 1990s.[7]

The basic economic question facing Mexico is the same one confronting a host of developing nations at similar points in their economic maturation: will Mexico during the next 10 years remain a country offering cheap labor to outside firms and suffering from recurrent currency crises, or will it take steps to build a robust and independent economy capable of long-term advancement? The answer depends first and foremost on sound macroeconomic policy and continued liberalization, but there are other factors essential to building a more diversified and competitive economy, particularly a modern small and medium-size business sector.

The economy's general composition is not far from that of industrial world economies. In 1995 services accounted for 64 percent of Mexico's GDP, while industry was at 28 percent and agriculture at 8 percent.[8] But although official unemployment rates remain in the single digits, underemployment is much higher—affecting a quarter or more of the population—and more than 10 percent of the population works for less than minimum wage.⁹ An even greater challenge to the Mexican economy is its large informal sector. Isolated from the modern economic foundation being laid by exports, the informal sector employs between a fifth and a third of the urban labor force. Meanwhile, self-employment accounts for more than 30 percent of the total workforce, compared to 25 percent in Spain and 10 percent in the United States. Drawing these informal and self-employed workers into the formal economy, where they can earn benefits while broadening the tax base, is a major task for the future.¹⁰

An Export-Driven Economy

Mexico's efforts to build a modern, export-oriented economy have made it one of the world's leading emerging market nations, advancing from the world's twenty-eighth largest exporter in 1980 to the tenth largest, with exports of more than $100 billion.¹¹ This growth in fact represents an even more impressive achievement than at first sight, because during this period the share of exports comprising oil dropped substantially and manufactured exports made up the difference. The most dynamic export sector is the *maquiladora* industry: the U.S.-Mexican border is one of the world's liveliest areas of economic development, growing at an annual rate of 7 percent or more and exporting in the neighborhood of $150 billion worth of goods. Throughout Mexico as a whole the number of exporting firms grew by almost half between 1993 and 1996, from 21,500 to 32,000. By 1996, Mexico's exports equalled 51.5 percent of GDP—almost double the G-7 average of 16.4 percent.¹² The head of one Mexican business group even suggested in 1997 that he could see a day coming when Mexico becomes "one of the four or five largest [international trade] players in the world, with US$300 billion in annual exports."¹³

Yet with few modern plants or domestic innovations, Mexico is largely a low-wage assembly point for parts imported from elsewhere. Intermediate goods—parts and components for automobiles, electronics, and other items assembled in Mexico—amount to 80 percent of the country's imports,¹⁴ indicating a stubborn and worrisome reality: that the country has yet to develop a broad-based manufacturing economy of its own. And with roughly three-quarters of its exports headed to a single destination, the United States, Mexico

Figure 16
Growth of Mexico's Exports and Foreign Direct Investment, 1980–1996

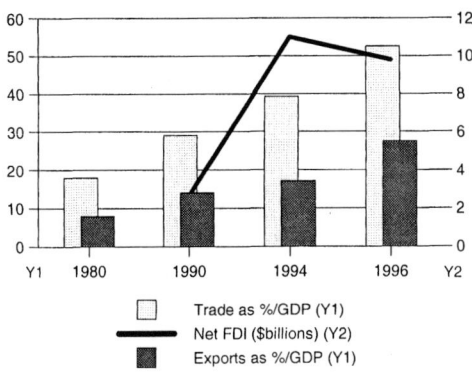

Source: Bank of Mexico.

Figure 17
Maquiladora Growth: Numbers and Growth Rate of Employed Workers, 1994–1997

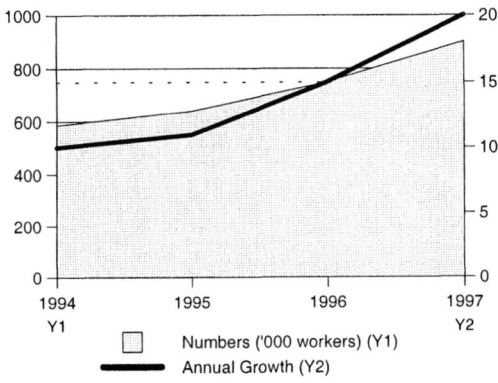

Source: Mexico, Office of the President (<www.presidencia.gob.mx>).

Figure 18
Mexico's Exports: Growth Rate and Share of World Exports

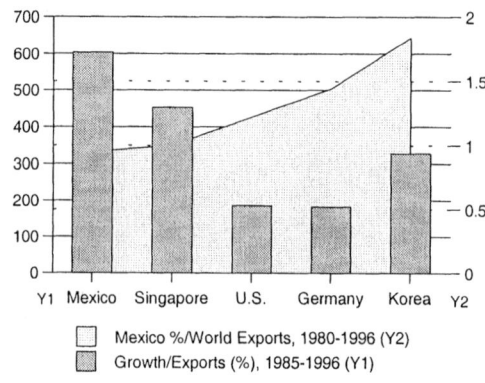

Source: Bank of Mexico (<www.banxico.org>).

remains vulnerable to dips in U.S. economic growth and changes in U.S. trade policy.

Advanced features of export-oriented businesses have yet to trickle down through the Mexican economy, for example, as seen in the level of technological sophistication in the business sector. In 1990 only 2.5 percent of Mexican manufacturing firms, and only 10 percent of large ones, used modern production technology. Research and development (R&D) expenditures stood at a meager 0.3 percent of GDP in 1993, compared to an OECD (Organization for Economic Cooperation and Development) average of 2.2 percent. What R&D takes place, moreover, is largely government-led; business research and development accounted for just 9 percent of Mexico's total in 1993, as opposed to an average of 60 percent in OECD countries.[15]

Also, although it is not generally emphasized, the bulk of Mexican exports come not from Mexican firms but from foreign firms operating in Mexico. No hard figures on this issue have been published, but a clue to their magnitude lies in the fact that 50 huge firms, many foreign-owned, account for 80 percent of Mexico's total exports.[16]

These are disturbing numbers for Mexico's future. Foreign investment provides jobs and thus helps to raise the national income, as well as providing tax receipts and other forms of economic support to the nation. But the corporate profits being made in Mexico today may benefit largely foreign shareholders.

Like nearly all developing economies, then, Mexico has used a dynamic export sector as a springboard to economic growth, foreign direct investment, and middle-class jobs for hundreds of thousands of workers. But Mexico's future competitiveness, like that of all countries that have passed through a similar stage of development, will depend on its ability to move beyond its current appeal as a site for low-wage manufacturing and assembly to a more diversified and integrated domestic economy. Meeting that goal requires, more than anything else, a competitive small and mid-size business sector.

Building a Diversified Economy: Small and Medium-Sized Firms

Apart from sensible macroeconomic policy to avoid the boom-and-bust cycles of past decades, the biggest challenge for the Mexican economy over the next decade is invigorating the country's small and medium-sized enterprises (SMEs). In the knowledge era, the role of smaller enterprises in fostering innovation, job creation, and growth is absolutely crucial, and Mexico probably cannot make the transition without vastly improving its SME sector. The health of SMEs is especially important from the standpoint of poverty, unemployment, and socioeconomic inequity, because smaller firms are often the ones that draw the less-skilled and less-well-off segments of the population into the workforce.

> Indeed, if one wants indicators of whether Mexico is developing a stable economic foundation, one could do worse than to look at the percentage of GDP and exports represented by small and medium-sized firms.

SMEs in Mexico face a host of barriers to enhanced competitiveness. Many have employees with low skill levels and managers without significant business training. Historically, miles of red tape have discouraged entrepreneurs wanting to develop or expand a new business.

The corrupting effects of the country's centralized political system have meant that large firms were favored in various ways. Few SMEs have understood the implications of new technologies for their business, and those that have often lack the funds to acquire them. Seeking high-quality inputs, larger Mexican firms have often looked abroad for goods in recent years: as of the 1990s, only 4 percent of Mexican microenterprises had a large local firm as their main client.[17] SMEs have largely been left out in the cold by Mexico's export surge.

Perhaps the most impenetrable barrier has been the lack of access to investment capital. In a sense the banks can hardly be blamed: few SMEs or microbusinesses are involved in the export chain; the average life span of microbusinesses in Mexico is three years; many of them operate in the informal sector of the economy; and 65 percent of those running microbusinesses say they have no interest in entrepreneurship and view their enterprises as a "transitory solution to lack of work."[18] The continued weakness of the banking sector is thus intimately related to the frailty of SMEs. Many domestic banks hold numerous bad loans and as a result have little new money to lend, but SMEs generally cannot gain access to international capital. This is one of the main reasons that SMEs have suffered at the hands of Mexico's liberalization drive. A handful of Mexican banks, such as Bital and Bancomer, are pushing aggressively into the SME market with good results, and their example may prompt other financial institutions to do likewise.

> "The vast majority of Mexican companies are small and medium-sized," reports the Economist Intelligence Unit, "and these often lack the capital or the know-how to counter foreign competition."[19] Until "this problem is addressed, periods of strong economic growth will be accompanied by widening trade and current accounts deficits."[20]

Once a stronger SME sector does begin to show itself, Mexico will graduate to a second-order problem, the same one faced by nearly all industrial nations: the lack of health and retirement benefits in small firms. As in the United States, very few Mexican SMEs offer such benefits, nor are they likely to, because of their small size. The requirements for business contributions to the new *afores* pension system, for example, would be onerous for many SMEs. The government should begin thinking today of solutions to this problem.[21]

The Service Sector

Mexico faces yet another daunting challenge as it considers the requirements of a knowledge-era economy: building a modern and competitive service sector. As in many other developing nations that have focused on manufactured exports, services in Mexico are poorly developed compared with the industrial sector. Both for the sake of domestic efficiency and for future export earnings, Mexico must give greater attention to nurturing competitive service industries. Residing next door to the world's largest service economy gives Mexico enviable opportunities to attract investment in dozens of newly traded service areas, from toll-free operators to information storage and Internet businesses.

Recent evidence gives the impression that the Mexican manufacturing sector is trying to become globally competitive and that the service sector has barely given much thought to the task. Economist Jonathan Heath explains that between June 1990 and April 1996, Mexico's manufacturing sector labored through "70 uninterrupted months of downsizing" and declining employment rolls, suggesting that the biggest companies began the process of re-engineering and retooling for global competition. During this same period, however, "retail and most small to-medium firms were not carrying out similar adjustments." By 1994 retail firms began to shed workers in the face of international competition, but the general message—that small and medium-sized service firms have a long road to competitiveness—remains disturbingly clear.[22] In fact, the proportion of the economy owned by the service sector is actually declining relative to manufacturing. Mexico's may be one of the few economies in the world to display this pattern, which is a result of the lack of competitiveness in the service sector.

The importance of a stronger service sector hints again at the interconnectedness of Mexico's economic challenges. Because many service businesses are SMEs, bolstering the service and SME sectors often amounts to the same thing. Because finance and capital is one of the most important components of the service sector, liberalizing

Issue Feature:
Bank Openness vs. Solvency—An Insoluble Dilemma?

The future of Mexico's banking system represents an intersection of several major trends under way in the country, from democratization to financial reform to economic openness. Like most such intersections, this one is rife with the potential to destabilize Mexican society over the next decade.

The first trend, or requirement, at work is the emergence of a healthier banking system from the ruins of the 1994 peso collapse. A stronger financial sector is absolutely indispensable to economic progress, and—although levels of bad loans remain disturbingly high—the capitalization level of banks in normal operations has nearly doubled since the end of 1994.[23]

But the recovery of Mexican banks may be increasingly imperiled by an intersecting trend: economic liberalization. As Mexico has allowed foreign banks to play a growing role in the country's financial sector, the competition facing domestic institutions has grown. Nearly two-thirds of total banking assets in the country reside in banks with a substantial foreign participation, damping down profits for Mexican firms and owners.[24]

Then there is a third trend—the democratization of Mexico. Opposition lawmakers, many in Congress, are demanding investigations of the bank bailouts overseen by the Mexican government after 1994. The government in 1998 proposed to convert some zero-interest bailout loans into public debt, and opponents claim corrupt bankers are being let off the hook with sweetheart deals. But gridlock over the bailout refinancing could keep the lid on bank lending, and thus economic growth.

Without expanded bank lending, Mexico's economic recovery will be short-lived; but without the kind of accountability promised by democratic oversight, secret financial deals could produce another financial collapse. The banking sector thus manifests the sort of wrenching dilemmas—and challenges for public policy—that Mexico will confront over the next decade.

Figure 19
Overdue Loan Ratio, Commercial Banks, 1989–1996

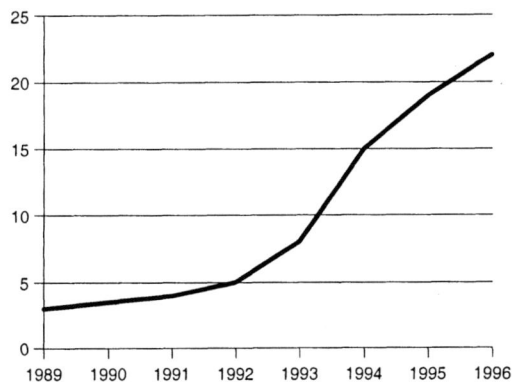

Source: Bank of Mexico, *The Mexican Economy 1997* (<www.banxico.org>).

Mexico's financial sector and bringing it out from under the crushing weight of bad loans are also imperative for its development.

Capital and Finance

Mexico is already a textbook example of the immense—and compassionless—power of global financial markets. The financial crisis of 1995 revealed the fickle, transitory character of modern investments. Some investors in Mexico, Andres Oppenheimer explains, with "no business history or long-term commitments in the country," bolted at the first sign of trouble, thus transforming a "bad situation into a far worse one."[25] The Asian financial crisis of 1997–1998 followed a similar pattern. To insulate itself from similar capital flight in the future, Mexico needs a stronger domestic economic base.

But the legacy of the recent crisis in Mexico, which has left many banks with large numbers of nonperforming loans, will make this goal much harder to achieve. The long-term costs of the banking problems have been estimated at between 10 and 12 percent of GDP, or about $40 billion—three to four times the relative impact of the

Figure 20
Gross Domestic Savings Rate, 1990-1996

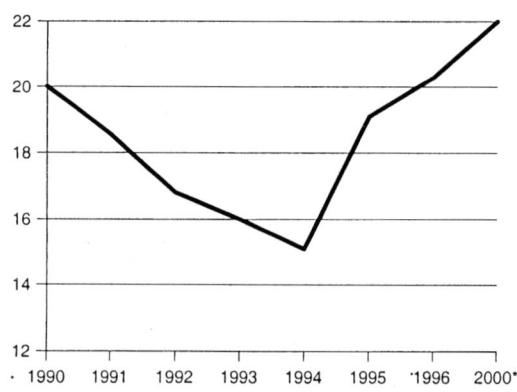

Sources: Bank of Mexico, *The Mexican Economy 1997* (Mexico City: Bank of Mexico, 1997), and OECD, *OECD Economic Surveys: Mexico* (Paris: OECD, 1996).

Note: Rate for 1996 from Bank of Mexico; all others are average of the two sources.
* Government target for year 2000.

U.S. savings and loan debacle.[26] Banks carrying bad loans have precious little capital to give out for new, productive business ventures.[27] One obvious route to capitalization is a higher national savings rate, and the government has this goal in its sights, setting a target of 22 percent of GNP in domestic savings by 2000, up from almost 16 percent in 1994. As of this writing, though, Mexican political leaders were deadlocked on the question of how to pay the more than $50 billion price tag for a domestic banking bailout—yet another example of the ways Mexico's nascent democracy complicates policymaking.

An important improvement for the outlook of the country's domestic capital markets was the pension reform that took effect in July 1997. Its goal was to mirror other Latin American success stories in Argentina and Chile by privatizing a substantial proportion of the country's retirement savings. Private pension fund companies, known as *afores*, will compete for investments, and Mexicans can choose their own funds. Contributions are automatic: the government will deduct 11.5 percent of workers' wages for transfer to the *afores*. The new system abandons the pay-as-you-go model, which is threatening to bankrupt many industrial nations as their baby boomers move into retirement years, and creates a system that will be self-financing. The government expected almost $5 billion to have been deposited by January 1998 and $10 billion by the end of that year, and it anticipates that nearly two and a half billion will be added per year for the next several years—a number that has the potential to rise considerably if the workforce adequately absorbs the numbers of young Mexicans reaching working age. Although the new system will not dramatically increase the national savings rate at first, partly because contributions have merely been shifted from the existing system, in the long run the habit and requirement for savings—and the higher returns achieved through competitive investments—could help boost savings rates.[28]

Socioeconomic Inequity

Inequality is a longstanding theme in Mexico, indeed, perhaps the most pervasive social issue in the country's history. A German visitor, Alexander von Humboldt, wrote in 1803 that "Mexico is the country of inequality," and the characterization is still fairly apt today. Succeeding in the knowledge era will demand close attention to this problem over the next decade and beyond. A "fundamental characteristic of the contemporary situation," observed Octavio Paz, is "the existence of two Mexicos, one modern and the other underdeveloped." This social bifurcation still presents the country with two pointed alternatives: "either the developed Mexico will absorb and integrate the other, or the underdeveloped Mexico, by the sheer dead weight and demographic increase, will end up by strangling the developed Mexico."[29]

The basic social dynamic of the knowledge era—driving a larger wedge between the knowledge-proficient and the knowledge-deprived—seems to be at work in Mexico. Globalization is opening up golden opportunities for a handful of management-level workers while drawing the majority of new workers into low-wage or menial positions. Wage differentials between skilled and unskilled workers "have widened by more than a quarter since 1990," the *Economist* notes,

**Figure 21
A Widening Gap: White- and Blue-Collar Real Hourly Wages, 1985–1995**
Index: 1980 = 100

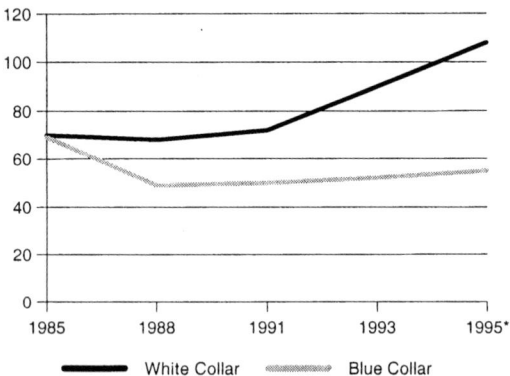

Source: OECD Country Survey: Mexico 1996.
* The 1995 figures predate the currency crisis, which undermined all wage levels.

creating wage gaps twice as large as in rich countries.[30] The Mexican middle class, Jorge Castañeda explains, is a minority of the population—about a quarter to a third of the total, compared with two-thirds in the United States. Meanwhile, the majority, "poor, urban, brown, and often without access to the main attributes of modern life . . . mingles with itself. It lives, works, sleeps, and worships apart from a small group of the very wealthy and a larger but still restricted middle class."[31]

The statistics on wealth inequity tell a disturbing story. One 1995 report concluded that

> it is widely known that 25 Mexican families control 54.2 percent of the nation's wealth, with half of Mexico's assets held by six conglomerates. . . . [T]he elite upper-tier absorbed an additional 0.6 percent of the nation's resources during the Salinas sexenio, whereas the poorest 20 percent lost 11 percent and now accounts for just 4.28 percent of the total economy. Except for Brazil, that is the greatest skew between haves and have-nots in Latin America.[32]

Issue Feature:
Hidden Evidence of Inequality

From the percentage of Mexicans living in poverty to the gap in income levels between those at the top and those at the bottom of the economic ladder, quantitative evidence of inequality in Mexico is not hard to find. In fact, the stark bifurcation of Mexican society along socioeconomic lines emerges in virtually every economic statistic.

The economist Jonathan Heath, for example, has shown how Mexico's true unemployment rate reflects the nation's disturbing degree of social inequity. Because Mexico offers no unemployment compensation and because few Mexican workers have substantial pools of savings, Health notes that "most Mexicans who are laid-off will immediately accept any job that comes along, including those that are demeaning and extremely low paid."

Taking the "official" unemployment figure at face value understates the problem. Mexico publishes an "alternative" unemployment figure, adding to the formally unemployed those who work for less than the minimum wage. Rather than 3.9 percent unemployment, the "official" figure for April 1997, this adjustment produces a rate of 22 percent.

Heath adds that the minimum wage has only 20 percent of the purchasing power it had two decades before; using the real minimum wage of 1976 as a guide, Heath finds that "more than 85 percent of the working force is either unemployed or earns less than a living wage." His conclusion: "Those Mexicans who have most of the purchasing power constitute the top 15 to 20 percent of the population."[33]

The character of the recovery in consumer spending paints the same portrait. Purchases of necessities such as food, clothing, and footwear continued to decline in 1996, while, according to the OECD, "purchases of household durables"—expensive items like dishwashers and refrigerators, "which represent only 10 percent of private consumption, concentrated in the higher income categories"—accounted for all the growth in consumer spending.[34]

The most obvious result of inequity is poverty. Recent measures of poverty vary, but all suggest that the situation remains unsatisfactory. In 1994 one estimate suggested that the top 10 percent of the population earned over 39 percent of national income and the bottom 10 percent just 1.6 percent.[35] Mexico's National Statistics Institute and the Banco de Mexico estimate that 68 million Mexicans, nearly three-quarters of the population, live in some degree of poverty. UNICEF recently found 9 million Mexican children living in "extreme poverty" and more than 60,000 living on the street.[36] More common estimates of the overall poverty rate run to about 40 percent, with extreme poverty at 20 percent or more; some reports suggest that two-thirds of Mexicans suffer from some level of malnutrition.[37] Regionally, in Chiapas, Hidalgo, Guerrero, and Oaxaca, incomes are 30 to 50 percent below the national average and 80 percent of the people living there have no access to safe drinking water.[38] That Mexico is also a country in which *Forbes* magazine counted 13 billionaires in the early 1990s—the fourth largest number of any country in the world, after the United States, Germany, and Japan[39]—speaks tellingly about the vast income inequities at work. The prevalence of billionaires amid poverty led writer Carlos Fuentes to describe Mexico as a country where 25 people earn the same as 25 million.[40]

Poverty and inequality are intimately connected to the country's prospects for developing a strong domestic market and thus a sound economy.

Most recent growth has been tied to exports; domestic demand per capita within Mexico has actually declined over the last two decades.[41] Without a reduction in poverty and an expansion of the middle class, Mexico will not be able to develop a strong domestic market, and its economic fortunes will remain chained to exports. "The principal defect in our industrialization," Octavio Paz recognized in the late 1960s, was "the weakness of our internal market."[42] This remains as true now as it was then, although there are a few signs of recovering domestic demand.

Broad-based economic growth is indispensable to meeting the challenge of socioeconomic inequity, but growth alone will not solve the problem. In fact, progress can be double-edged if added wealth

Surprise Scenario:
U.S. War on Immigration

Immigration, both legal and illegal, is a thorn in the side of U.S.-Mexican relations. The hope is that this irritant will be dislodged by economic progress in Mexico—another way in which the success or failure of economic progress can have ripple effects throughout society, politics, and even foreign relations.

But there is an alternative scenario, the product of the interaction of demography and economics. What if Mexico cannot provide the one million jobs a year needed to bring its younger people into the workforce? What if it is unable to provide even a fraction of those jobs? In this case desperation and the hope for a better life might propel tens of thousands more young Mexicans into the United States, precipitating a harsh U.S. reaction.

This scenario raises the implications of a new war on illegal immigration waged by the United States in response to a large influx across its southern border. The aim of this new policy would be to erect a sort of impregnable "wall" at the border to staunch the flow of illegals. This outcome appears exceedingly unlikely today, given the growing clout of Latino voters, but it cannot be ruled out in the case of a U.S. recession or major instability in Mexico.

Such a move would be provocative and counterproductive. It is, however, politically conceivable. Some implications might be

- **Immediate and severe worsening of Mexican-U.S. relations.** Mexico would vehemently protest the action, and recent efforts to put relations on a sounder footing would come to naught.

- **Social instability in Mexico.** As would-be immigrants could neither get out of the country nor find jobs at home, their reaction suddenly could even become violent. Some observers describe an end to immigration as the single most destabilizing scenario imaginable for Mexico's society and economy.

- **A radicalization of Mexican politics.** Nationalists and old-guard PRI leaders may use the issue as a rallying point to renew a larger role for the state in the economy.

only sharpens the challenge of economic distribution and creates a need for the government to provide a consistently rising standard of living for all. Economic advancement is already enfranchising a highly educated, technologically oriented, and entrepreneurial middle class in Mexico, but it is still a relatively small proportion of the population and its prospects for growth depend on the country's prospects for stable and sustainable development.

One estimate, for example, puts the middle class at over 21 million people, a fourth of the population, with a per capita income of $10,000.[43] Others see this estimate as exaggerated, suggesting that the country's real consumer class is just 10 to 20 percent of the total, with less than 20 percent its members enjoying a per capita income of $7,000 or more.[44] Either way, Mexico obviously has a long way to go before it becomes a thoroughly middle-class country, with 60 percent or more of the population in that category, as in the United States.

Institutionalizing the Recovery

Finally, it is worth stressing the connection between Mexico's economic future and its requirement to build reliable, trusted institutions of governance. Mexico could make the same mistakes today that led to the peso collapse in 1995, because economic decisionmaking remains so personalized. The "profound lessons" of the peso crisis, Carlos Fuentes has explained, are that "while it may have manifested itself in the economy, it has its roots—and a solution—in politics."[45] The presidency is dominant, and efforts to create more powerful finance ministries and central banks and to enhance the professionalism of institutions like Bancomex and Secofi are to be lauded and must be pushed further. Strengthening the centers of economic decisionmaking outside the presidency is an urgent priority—just as, in the broader sense, building the institutions of a democracy is a precondition for success on a number of fronts. Mexico must exchange its "government of men" for a government of laws and institutions; as the *Economist* has observed, democracy, "by promising to end the grip of one-party politics on the economy, offers the only real hope that Mexico can break free of its ugly economic cycles and uglier crises."[46]

The new pension arrangement reinforces the interconnectedness of a rule-of-law society with other social goals, including a healthy financial sector. Pumping new savings into the system is a necessary, but insufficient, condition for stability; equally important is the strengthening of financial accountability and transparency laws. Until it is anchored in a stronger legal system, Mexico's financial sector will continue to rest on a quicksand of backroom dealings and lack of accountability. In sum, the Mexican economy is jetting ahead, fueled by foreign investment and exports, but its recent success is built on a weak foundation. The next decade will determine whether it is ready to turn the corner toward stronger economic fundamentals.

Notes

1. Walter Wriston, *The Twilight of Sovereignty* (New York: Scribner's, 1992), 5.
2. Cited in Jeremy Rifkin, *The End of Work* (New York: G. P. Putnam's Sons, 1995), 190–191.
3. See James F. Moore, *The Death of Competition: Leadership and Strategy in the Age of Business Ecosystems* (New York: HarperBusiness, 1996), 3, 11–12, 15.
4. See Sheldon Danziger and Peter Gottschaulk, *America Unequal* (Cambridge: Harvard University Press, 1995); Rifkin, *The End of Work*, 169–177; and Kevin Phillips, *Boiling Point: Democrats, Republicans, and the Decline of Middle-Class Prosperity* (New York: Random House, 1993).
5. Cited in the *Washington Post,* February 3, 1997, p. A6.
6. World Bank, *Global Economic Prospects and the Developing Countries* (Washington, D.C.: World Bank, 1995), 63.
7. Andres Oppenheimer, *Bordering on Chaos: Guerrillas, Stockbrokers, Politicians, and Mexico's Road to Prosperity* (Boston: Little, Brown and Company, 1996), 152.
8. World Bank, *Trends in Developing Economies 1996* (Washington, D.C.: World Bank, 1996), 340.
9. Economist Intelligence Unit, *Mexico 1996–1997* (London: EIU, 1996), 48.
10. OECD, *Economic Surveys: Mexico* (Paris: OECD, 1996), 72–73, 86.
11. Bank of Mexico, *The Mexican Economy 1997*, chap. 9, "Structural Change in the External Sector of the Mexican Economy," <www.banxico.org>.

12. OECD, *Environmental Performance Review: Mexico* (Paris: OECD, 1998), 42.
13. Jeff Jones, "Are Exports Unlimited?" *Business Mexico*, June 1997, 12.
14. Economist Intelligence Unit, *Mexico 1996–1997*, 38, and *Mexico: Third Quarter 1997* (London: EIU, 1997), 5.
15. OECD, *Economic Surveys: Mexico*, 107–108. But see also Geri Smith and Elisabeth Malkin, "Mexican Makeover," *Business Week*, December 21, 1998, 50–52.
16. Jones, "Are Exports Unlimited," 13.
17. OECD, *Economic Surveys: Mexico*, 110.
18. Richard Byrd, "Loan Rangers: Too Few Banks Willing to Lend to Small Enterprise," *Business Mexico*, September 1997, 20.
19. Economist Intelligence Unit, *Mexico 1996–1997*, 32.
20. Economist Intelligence Unit, *Mexico: Fourth Quarter 1997* (London: EIU, 1997), 9.
21. A related challenge is environmental: as ecological regulations toughen in Mexico, some SMEs will face substantial up-front costs in environmental treatment technology. One estimate suggests that just 30 percent of SMEs have environmental technology that measures up even to Mexico's so-far poor national standards in this area. Brian Feagans, "Green Lights," *Business Mexico*, September 1997, 38.
22. Jonathan Heath, "The Costs and Benefits of Mexico's Transformation," *Washington Quarterly* 20, no. 4 (Autumn 1997): 144.
23. OECD, *Economic Surveys: Mexico 1997–1998* (Paris: OECD, 1998), 82.
24. Ibid., 87.
25. Oppenheimer, *Bordering on Chaos*, 54.
26. Shahid Javed Burki and Guillermo E. Perry, *The Long March: A Reform Agenda for Latin America and the Caribbean in the Next Decade* (Washington, D.C.: World Bank, 1997), 9. In 1997 Mexico's National Banking and Securities Commission and Finance Secretariat revised their estimates of the bailout into this range. Jeff Wright, "For Sale: For Better or for Worse," *Business Mexico*, October 1997, 10.
27. The OECD, for example, concludes that the banking sector remains "fragile" and will become more robust only when the economic recovery "has become more firmly based and reaches out across sectors beyond exporting firms." OECD, *Economic Surveys: Mexico*, 60.
28. Some observers have worried that the new pension system is in fact not completely competitive and divorced from the political realm insofar as a government-run afore will compete with others and even has some

oversight responsibilities for them. And there are substantial unfunded liabilities, namely, huge amounts of benefits owed to current and imminent retirees who will not benefit from the new system. Some estimates put the sum of those liabilities as high as 80 percent of gross domestic product. The costs, of course, will not be borne all at once: 1997's tab is anticipated to be 0.5 percent of GDP. And if the scheme is even partly successful, Mexico will have jumped in well ahead of its aging curve, long before it would face a European-, U.S.-, or Japanese-style crisis of a pay-as-you-go pension system. Ian Vasquez, "Two Cheers for Mexico's Pension Reform," *Wall Street Journal*, June 27, 1997.

29. Octavio Paz, *The Labyrinth of Solitude and Other Writings*, trans. Lysander Kemp, Yara Milos, and Rachel Phillips Belash (New York: Grove Press, 1985), 260.

30. "Great Reforms, Nice Growth, But Where Are the Jobs?" *Economist*, March 21, 1998, 37. According to a 1998 World Bank report, Mexico has more people in poverty (75 percent of the total) than all but three other nations in the world. World Bank, *World Development Indicators 1998* (Washington, D.C.: World Bank, 1998), 5.

31. Jorge G. Castañeda, "Ferocious Differences," *Atlantic*, July 1995; available at <www.theatlantic.com>.

32. Joan Rothman, "The New Sexenio," *Global Marketing* 3, no. 4 (1995): 41.

33. Heath, "Costs and Benefits," 145.

34. OECD, *Economic Surveys: Mexico 1997–1998*, 20.

35. Economist Intelligence Unit, *Mexico 1996–1997*, 16.

36. Nicholas Wilson, "What's Wrong with This Picture?" *Business Mexico*, April 1997, 22.

37. Rothman, "The New Sexenio," and Sidney Weintraub, "The Complex Situation That Is Mexico," *Washington Quarterly* 20, no. 4 (Autumn 1997): 97–98.

38. Economist Intelligence Unit, *Mexico 1996–1997*, 18.

39. Oppenheimer, *Bordering on Chaos*, 8.

40. Wilson, "What's Wrong with This Picture?" 23.

41. Ibid.

42. Paz, *Labyrinth of Solitude*, 259.

43. Paula Kephart, "Middle-Class on $10,000 a Year," *American Demographics*, September 1994, 15.

44. Wilson, "What's Wrong with This Picture?" 22.

45. Carlos Fuentes, *A New Time for Mexico* (Berkeley: University of California Press, 1996), 131.

46. "The Lingering Tequila Hangover," *Economist*, March 14, 1998, 17.

4 ■
Trend Four: An Era of Global Tribes

THE KNOWLEDGE ERA is a time of paradox and contradiction, a time when theses and antitheses meld to produce unexpectedly powerful engines of social change. Conflicting trends gain speed at the same time, pulling societies in two or more directions. Nowhere is this more evident than in one of the greatest paradoxes of our time: the simultaneous acceleration of globalism and pluralism, which is producing what might be called "global tribes." The world is at once becoming both more cosmopolitan and more insular; expanding global trade, communication, and travel arouse a deeper interest in local, national, ethnic, and religious identities. And all too often, the forces of globalism have an uneasy relation to the local, tribal, national, and individual reactions they inspire.

The Process of Globalization

To say that "globalization" is one of the most overused phrases of our time does not deny the reality of the process it describes: the increasing convergence of the world's economies and societies. But globalization is not a uniform phenomenon; it is more pronounced in some areas, and less in others.

To begin with, the world economy is increasingly globalized. Trade in merchandise and services is growing faster than worldwide economic growth, which means that the world economy is more dependent on trade, and thus more globalized, with each passing year. The

Figure 22
World Trade Integration, 1972-2002
Export plus import merchandise trade volumes as share of GDP

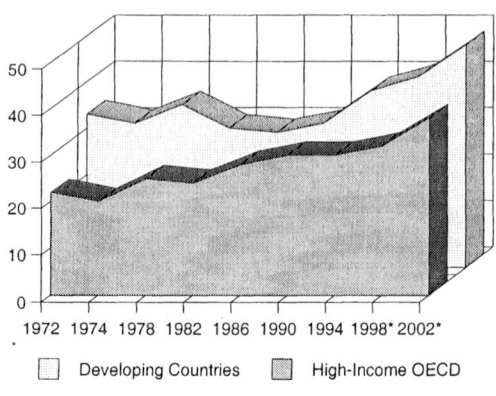

Source: World Bank, *Global Economic Prospects and the Developing Countries* (Washington, D.C.: World Bank, 1995).
* Figures for 1998 and 2002 are projections.

World Bank forecasts that this trend will continue over the next decade, so that by the year 2004 global trade levels will be equivalent to just under half of the world's GDP.

In many ways, though, this economic activity retains a highly regional focus. The majority of world trade (and a majority that continues to grow) goes on within each of the three major trading blocs—Europe, the Americas, and East Asia—rather than between them. Between 1985 and 1993 U.S. exports and imports from North America grew relative to trade in other areas; EU trade within Europe grew relative to other trade; and Japanese trade within East Asia rose relative to other trade. In Europe intraregional trade accounts for almost 70 percent of the total. The trends are similar for foreign investment.[1]

Over the next decade, a second major avenue of globalization will be global awareness. There is an emerging tendency toward global consciousness—a shorthand description of the trend toward homogenization discussed in chapter 2. This global mentality is evident in increasingly specialized professions, whose members may have more in common with colleagues halfway around the world than with their own neighbors.

Third, and perhaps most important, globalization will speed up over the next decade as a result of advances in communications. The *Economist* recently summarized the direction of global communications technologies:

> Over the next few years, the price of making a long-distance call in and between some countries will fall to the point where it costs little more to telephone from Hollywood to Glasgow than to nearby Beverly Hills. At the same time, telephone companies will begin to switch the basis of charging their customers from the length of time for which they talk to a flat subscription. Within a decade or two, most ordinary telephone conversations will cost nothing extra, whatever their duration or distance.

This process will revolutionize service activities, recalibrate cost calculations, and "may well prove the most significant economic force shaping the next half century."[2]

Fourth, a globalized world is characterized by global production, or the rise of multinational corporations. By the early 1990s there were 37,000 parent multinationals controlling 206,000 foreign affiliate corporations.[3] Amazingly, as long ago as 1992, the total sales of foreign affiliates operated by multinational corporations were $5.5 trillion, more than five times the value of world exports that year. This fact suggests that multinational corporations may already be a much more powerful engine of globalization than traditional trade in manufactured goods and services. Meanwhile, other aspects of the knowledge era are working to transcend the distinction between global and local companies. In a world of virtual companies and networked alliances distributed around the globe, each doing its business with intense local and niche focus but coordinating and trading globally, the emerging model is a paradoxical one.

Tribalism, Fragmentation, and Pluralism

If a knowledge era is a time of globalism, it is also, paradoxically, an era of pluralism—of fragmentation in social organization; diversity in careers, politics, and religion; a renewed search for identity in local, tribal, and national contexts. The knowledge era is pluralistic for a number of reasons; it draws on and expands the natural pluralism of modern industrial society, with its hundreds of careers and millions of products. The difference is that we now have access, through information and global marketing, to this dizzying array of options.

The business world is fragmenting as well. In a fast-moving, pluralistic era, it hardly seems surprising that smaller and more decentralized corporations have an edge in flexibility and innovation. But the story is not that simple: in important sectors of the economy, massive size and scope rather than fragmentation are the rule. That a trend toward bigness should emerge alongside the growing importance of small business is another symptom of a paradoxical time. The central message for businesses, then, is not so much big versus small as the effort to be both at once. The corporate challenge today, says Louis Gerstner of IBM, is "how to incorporate small-company attributes—nimbleness, speed, and customer responsiveness—with the advantages of size."[4] Successful businesses will combine, either within their own organization or through alliances and networks, small- and big-company attributes, along with characteristics of both local and global operations.

Tribalism within Globalism

Pluralism and universalism, tribalism and globalism, are each important in their own right. But even more decisive is their interaction, the complex and profound dynamic of a world that is not merely global, but plurally global; not merely plural, but globally plural. In short, major implications for the coming decade are to be found at the intersection of these two trends.

The writer Patrick Glynn predicts a coming clash between "ethnic (and other types of) particularism" and "what might be called democratic universalism." This impending conflict "seems to be replacing the old Left-Right and class polarities that have governed political life for nearly a century." The contest between pluralism and globalism, which "has every appearance of becoming the new bipolarity of global politics, the new dialectic of a new age,"[5] has a number of ramifications. One is social instability, tension, or outright

Issue Feature:
Examples of Pluralism

The pluralism of the knowledge era will emerge in dozens of ways, in fields as diverse as politics and currency and art, and in a manner that is more comprehensive and fundamental than at any previous time in human history. This issue feature offers just a few examples of the fragmented, decentralized, personalized character of the knowledge era.

■ Self-identification. A recent survey by *U.S. News and World Report* found that the political attitudes of Americans had broken down into seven "tribes," including populist traditionalists, stewards, dowagers, liberal activists, and agnostics.[6]

■ The multicultural movement. One of the most important social trends of our time, multiculturalism—which rejects a universal lifestyle in favor of regional or ethnic distinctions—is tribalism on display.

■ The fragmentation of business. The decentralization and "virtualization" of business is also a form of pluralism.

■ The diversification of education and justice. Both institutions display a bewildering array of specialized schools, subjects, classes, style of law enforcement, and forms of punishment and rehabilitation.

■ Government decentralization. The movement in the United States, Western Europe, and elsewhere toward devolving government affairs to lower levels of authority is an example of pluralism.

■ The fragmenting effects of media. In a world of 150-channel cable television and almost unlimited online, print, and broadcast media options, the public becomes a "segmented, differentiated audience," no longer "a mass audience in terms of simultaneity and uniformity of the message it receives."[7]

■ A pluralism of religions. In a time of diversity, religious forces become less monolithic and encompassing, more local and diverse.

conflict in many areas of the world. This process, after all, is the engine of the clash of cultures as described by Samuel Huntington. "The forces of integration in the world are real," he writes, "and are precisely what are generating counterforces of cultural assertion."[8] But at the same time, globalism in all its guises enhances interdependence among and within nations.

Mexico and the Global-Tribal Intersection

In this increasingly global and local era, Mexico confronts the same issues of identity, belonging, and competitiveness as most other people in the world today. At a 1997 conference, when a group of Mexican government officials and corporate executives were asked to identify the greatest change in their lives during the past decade, the unanimous answer was "globalization."[9]

> But there is some reason to hope that Mexico can deal with globalization and its implications—including the countervailing trend of pluralism or tribalism—more effectively than many other developing nations, fashioning a more comfortable blend of local culture and global values.

Latin America, Mexico included, was already deeply affected by the world's first tide of "globalization," the Western Hemisphere's conquest by European powers. The racial and cultural mixing that is so much a part of Mexico's heritage represents the country's first global-tribal intersection and continues to be a vital source of Mexican culture. Having successfully produced a robust national identity from these roots, Mexico and its people may be uniquely confident of the country's ability to do so again. At the same time, Mexico will hardly be immune to the intense social strains imposed by globalization throughout the rest of the world; without careful attention, globalization could render permanent Mexico's stark cleavage between rich and poor, drawing a small minority of educated businesspeople into the world economy while leaving tens of millions of disenfranchised Mexicans in a condition of hopeless poverty.

Engines of Globalization

Probably the most powerful measure of the degree to which Mexico has been globalized in recent years is its role as one of the world's

Issue Feature:
Global-Local Tensions at the Border

The U.S.-Mexican border is a powerful symbol of globalization's impact on economic and social life, along with local, national, and tribal reactions to it. More than 2,000 miles long and 130 miles wide, this slice of two countries boasts a population of 11 million people and a GDP of $150 billion. **If the border were a country, it would have one of the largest economies in the developing world**, ahead of Poland's and just behind Thailand's.[10] It is growing at an annual rate of 7 percent, more quickly than Mexico or the United States as a whole.

Mexico ranks second to China as a destination for developing-world investment. There are close to 2,000 *maquiladoras* in the border region. Tijuana produces 14 million television sets a year, more than any place else in the world. **The list of international investors in the border region reads like a who's who of global automotive and electronics giants:** Sanyo (which moved its U.S. headquarters from New York to San Diego), Samsung (building a $700 million electronic factory), Daewoo, Sony, Hitachi, Matsushita. General Motors' Delphi Automotive Division has a massive research center in Cuidad Juárez, employing mostly Mexican engineers and operating 24 hours a day.

One result has been an homogenization of attitudes. Border residents may "pick up American political ideas," *Business Week* suggests, which helps to explain the success of free market-oriented PAN candidates in the north. Mexican managers are also exposed to global influences. One recently delivered his business card to reporters with an Asian-style bow, remarking: "I've been to Asia so often and received so many Asian investors here, it has become second nature to me."

The process also has broader social impacts. As *Business Week* observes, "a class of skilled Mexicans . . . is rising to the fore to run the hundreds of new plants." That's good as far as it goes, but it also risks creating new social divisions: most of the workers are low-paid migrants from elsewhere in Mexico who reside in shantytowns. Along with the benefits of commerce, **globalization's more sinister progenies are also present:** an expanded drug trade and a lively "body trade" in illegal immigrants. Keeping these dangers in check while nurturing the border's opportunities represents Mexico's global-local challenge in a nutshell.

fastest-growing export economies. Like the world economy as a whole, Mexico's economy is heavily tied to trade and will become more so in the years to come. Public enthusiasm for open trade is substantial; in 1990, 80 to 85 percent of Mexicans polled in the world values survey expressed support.[11] Even if one assumes that the government helped to inflate these numbers with its pro-NAFTA campaigns, they remain impressive. As much as any other developing nation Mexico reflects the globalizing influence of two economic trends: interwoven worldwide financial markets and globally active multinational corporations.

With easy access to information from abroad, substantial portions of the Mexican population already reflect the sort of global consciousness that typifies advanced economies. World values surveys and other polls have demonstrated what seems to be a convergence in attitudes between Mexico and its North American NAFTA partners, the United States and Canada. Perhaps especially because Mexico's larger younger generations are influenced by U.S. consumerist, democratic, individualistic, and achievement-oriented values, the country reflects a homogeneous, globalized consciousness of the sort on display throughout the world. "A narrow nationalism that had been dominant since the nineteenth century," Inglehart, Nevitte, and Basañez contend, "is gradually giving way to a more cosmopolitan sense of identity" in Mexico as well as the United States and Canada.[12]

Mexico seems to be further along in embracing these values than many other developing nations. Extensive public opinion polls reveal that Mexico already ranks as one of the most modern countries in Latin America in terms of its social values. On Ronald Inglehart's scale of "materialist" and "postmaterialist" values—with the first set of values generally characteristic of poor countries where material needs are not reliably met, and the second set characteristic of wealthier countries where people have few fears about their basic needs and shift their concerns to secondary issues, such as freedom—Mexico stands out as the most postmaterialist nation in Latin America.[13]

Mexico's middle class is young, technology-savvy, and thus more likely to welcome influences from advanced nations. A 1993 survey found that the average resident of Mexico City was more likely to view computers, stereos, and VCRs as "essential" equipment than residents of the United States were (on computers, for example, the

Figure 23
Postmaterialist Values in Mexico
National scores on "postmaterialist values index"

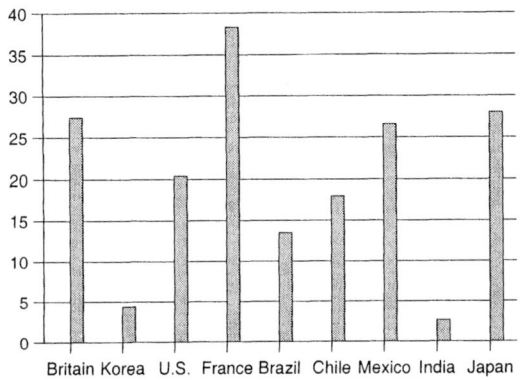

Source: Paul R. Abramson and Ronald F. Inglehart, *Value Change in Global Perspective* (Ann Arbor: University of Michigan Press, 1995), 124.

difference was 85 percent to 36 percent). This makes Mexico a hot market for high-technology goods: 85 percent of households have a television set, and the country has one of the fastest-growing cellular phone markets in the world.[14]

Economically, culturally, and politically, then, Mexico should be at home in an increasingly global world. Of course, like many developing nations, it has a long way to go before becoming a full-fledged member of the knowledge era. As of 1996 it still had only 70 telephones per 1,000 inhabitants—industrial nations average between 400 and 500—to say nothing of the famously poor quality and unreliability of the Mexican telephone system.[15] But these numbers will rise dramatically over the next 10 years, drawing Mexico much further into the knowledge era and spreading global awareness. The question is whether this process will apply mostly to the well-off, driving an even bigger wedge between rich and poor, or whether the knowledge revolution—an empowering, egalitarian force in the industrial world—can have the same beneficent effects in a country as unequal as Mexico.

Regionalism, Not Globalism—and with a Yankee Face

And yet, as the example of northern Mexico illustrates, at issue is not—at least not yet—globalization so much as integration with the United States. Mexico's economic, political, and cultural engagement of the outside world is not diversified. It depends heavily on contacts with its huge northern neighbor: its trade is dominated by the United States on both the import and export side; information pouring into Mexico from abroad comes largely from U.S. sources; and half of the Mexican population know someone who lives across the border while one-third have a family member who has traveled there. This reflects a pattern of regionalism with unique and troublesome implications for Mexico.

Throughout Mexican life, Jorge Castañeda worried a decade ago, "the American presence is overwhelming." He predicted that an acceleration of that influence—just the sort under way now in the age of NAFTA—would "threaten the [Mexican] nation's very soul," because the weight of U.S. economic superiority in the relationship "can be crushing and can lead to a permanent loss of significant attributes of sovereignty and cultural identity."[16] In Andres Oppenheimer's words, the country is "hiding its national reality behind the mask of an Americanization process that gave it a false illusion of prosperity"; the Chiapas rebel leader, Subcommander Marcos, offered to take off his signature ski mask "if Mexican society takes off the mask that those with alien vocations have placed on it."[17]

Even with this intensely felt issue, however, there is reason for hope that Mexico can successfully manage its own American-tinted version of the global-local dynamic. Attitudes in Mexico toward the United States are not as negative as is commonly assumed, especially among the young. Miguel Basañez has described anti-Americanism in Mexico as a "myth." "The idea of a fervent nationalism and anti-Americanism, " he says, "has been exploited by the Mexican government," but it is "not supported by the facts."[18] Even Castañeda, tacitly recognizing the underlying engines of history surveyed in chapter 2, asks whether

> the relative uniformity of fashion, eating habits, television fare, music popularity, and movies throughout the world is a symptom

of Americanization, or does it simply constitute an expression of U.S. influence in an increasingly unified, global, and mainly middle-class-oriented cultural marketplace? Are blue jeans American, or middle-class? . . . Are fast-food joints a product of American hegemony, or the result of more women in the workplace with less time to cook?

All of these things are seen as "American," Castañeda suggests, "only because the United States is the quintessential middle-class country, which all others are increasingly resembling, whether they like it or not." Thus "the 'Americanization' of Mexico should perhaps be seen more correctly as the 'modernization' of Mexico," and he finally pronounces himself satisfied that Americanization (or modernization) poses a limited threat, because "Mexico possesses an extraordinarily rich, diversified, historically well-anchored cultural personality of its own." "All the McDonald's in the world," he says, "could never submerge" these traditions.[19]

Thus Mexico may well be on the way toward a successful integration of global and local values, norms, and habits. Its historical experiences, the cultural and ethnic mix of its people, its widespread youthful exuberance about global influences it sees at work—these and other factors suggest that Mexico may be able to manage the tensions of a paradoxically global and plural era better than many other developing (and industrial) nations, in both the short and long terms.

But globalization has its price in Mexico as elsewhere. Even a nation attuned to its potential advantages and nuances will face social dislocations as it becomes "globalized."

For one thing, globalization—at least in its early phases—could easily worsen social inequities by pouring wealth into the hands of a relatively small, highly educated class while shunting aside millions of less-skilled workers. The challenge to employment will be especially severe as liberalization continues and foreign competition enters one sector after another, including, ultimately, services. To combat such trends, old-guard politicians may well inflame nationalistic, xenophobic, and protectionist sentiments. Hints of this were apparent in Mexican government policies toward foreign human rights activists and foreign companies in 1998.

More anecdotally, some young Mexicans returning from the United States—or from Mexican theaters showing films about the United States—are determined to mimic the most vicious aspects of U.S. gang culture. Americans commonly think of Mexico as a trans-shipment point for drugs and violence entering the United States, but the reverse is increasingly true. One observer has described the frightening trend among Mexican youth in one Mexico City suburb:

> [They] have introduced a semblance of *la vida loca*, the crazy life, of U.S. young-gang culture. They've rechristened their neighborhoods with street names from Los Angeles: 18 Street, Echo Park, Florencia. They listen to rap music in English and try to act as hard as a gangsta from Compton, and in fact recently perpetrated their first drive-by shootings against rival gangs.[20]

If Mexico fails to engender a virtuous economic cycle—that is, if large numbers of young Mexicans reach working age only to find themselves shut out of the productive economy—thousands of them could turn to the growing U.S.-style gang movement for identity and money. The gangs would become yet another form of social disorder undermining the stability of Mexican society.

The Contrary Trend: Pluralism and Tribalism

Mexico also reflects the rise of pluralism and tribalism, in contrast to (and sometimes in reaction to) the trend toward globalization. Socially, Mexico has been a pluralistic country for much of its history and is becoming more so all the time. Politically and economically, pluralism in Mexico takes a number of forms, most notably an intense regionalism and devolution of government power. In the medium term, Mexico also may face, and perhaps benefit from, fundamental kinds of radical decentralization characteristic of the knowledge era.

For example, slowly but unmistakably decentralization is coming to Mexican politics. It is a major element on the PAN agenda. In the state of Guanajuato, Governor Vicente Fox Quesada has pursued a three-part devolution plan, demanding more state control from Mexico City while also pushing more functions, responsibilities, and powers down to municipalities and citizens.[21] How far this process will go is open to question, at least in the medium term. The traditional dominance of Mexico City and the presidency militate against a more decentralized system. But the trend in that direction is obvious, and the first stage of local empowerment is in sight.

> At the same time, as governmental authority becomes more decentralized it is acquiring a more regional flavor. Some worry that regional differences will become more pronounced, to the point of endangering the country's long-term unity.

In a situation mirroring the regional split in Italy, Mexico's northern states believe that they are subsidizing the south, a belief expressed in electoral victories for the right-of-center PAN. Joined with sympathy for the left-leaning PRD in the south, this trend may ultimately "call into question Mexico's long-term prospects for territorial integrity and political stability."[22] Ethnic cleavages exacerbate these trends: Mexico today has a larger population of Indians than it did in 1910—although their percentage in the overall population has declined—and they are concentrated heavily in the southern parts of the country.

Yet the drift toward a destructive regionalism may not necessarily continue. For one thing, both the PAN and the PRD aspire to be truly national parties, competitive across the country in presidential elections. Both have an incentive therefore to avoid strictly regional agendas and to appeal to new constituencies—the PAN in the south, the PRD in the north. Moreover, the PAN may be more of an urban party than a northern one, and southern cities increasingly have more in common with their northern counterparts than either have with rural areas. This would fragment the strict north-south dichotomy. Indeed, a rural-urban split, supported by a substantial divergence in wealth and income, may well be more important than regional divisions in the twenty-first century.

> Some Mexicans worry that, with the decline of traditional forms of authority, Mexican society, and especially its young, will reflect another aspect of knowledge-era pluralism: the relativism of moral values.

All nations that have, in the process of modernization, shed traditional or hierarchical values and institutions in favor of more open,

Issue Feature:
Carlos Fuentes and the Global-Local Paradox

As a perceptive new biography by Maarten van Delden recounts, the famed Mexican writer Carlos Fuentes has embodied the tension between global and national identity in the Mexican psyche. Fuentes became a citizen of the world early on: the son of a diplomat, he traveled throughout the hemisphere. Yet he has never stopped being thoroughly Mexican, and this mixture has influenced his thinking.

As van Delden explains, in the 1950s, as co-editor of the *Revista Mexicana de Literatura,* Fuentes tried to "develop and defend a cosmopolitan view of Mexican culture" by publishing "an attack on literary and cultural nationalism." He perceived himself as a "figure who must break free of his cultural roots in order to become part of an elite, supranational community." Yet at the same time, Fuentes has "staked out a position as a fiery spokesman for Mexican and Latin American independence."

This has meant that Fuentes "acknowledges the inevitability of the current process of globalization" and favors Mexico's economic liberalization, but retains "serious reservations" about the implications of these trends and insists that Mexico safeguard its sovereignty and the well-being of its poor. While he agrees that "the encounter with the other is the great drama of our time and the time to come," he is uncertain of its outcome: because it leads to "a more intense consciousness of one's own identity," it reflects Fuentes's ambiguity about "the will to transcend cultural boundaries, and the desire to safeguard them."

In the final analysis, Fuentes stands for the hope that Mexico—and all nations in the knowledge era—can reconcile a globalist cosmopolitanism with their rich cultural traditions. He "has developed a vision of contemporary culture," van Delden observes, "as essentially global and multicultural in nature."[23] In Fuentes' own words: "How shall we wed the local values of identity with the universal values of communication?" The answer: by pursuing, not "exclusionary modernity" that "banishes all that it does not understand," but rather, "inclusive modernity," which understands "that there are many ways of being 'modern,' of being contemporaneous with one's own values."[24]

inclusive, democratic (and, some worry, permissive) standards of behavior have faced the same challenge: that of recreating the foundations of a social ethic almost from scratch. The challenge is to do this without abandoning the idea of ethical or moral standards altogether; indeed, the transition to the knowledge era renders the moral and spiritual dimension of social life and public policy more important than ever. In the maelstrom of social change that is sure to hit Mexico over the next decade, young people will need a new moral compass. It is not clear, at this point, where they will find it.

Pluralism will also be on display in the form of a decentralization of business strategies. Multinational corporations have already had to adjust their local operations to Mexican cultural standards. Increasingly, world-class Mexican companies will employ the same kind of micromarketing and niche advertising as companies around the world. Corporations in Mexico will have to become increasingly local even as they gain global awareness and operations.

Pluralism within Globalism: The Mexican Style

The collision of globalism and tribalism or pluralism is expected to produce severe social tensions around the world over the next decade—social instability, protectionism, trade wars, even the "clash of civilizations" forecast by Samuel Huntington. But there is reason to hope that Mexico can better navigate the intersection of global knowledge and economics with national and local cultures than many other developing and industrial nations can. Mexicans have confronted this dilemma for hundreds of years and in the process have managed to construct a solid national identity and sense of self. They see in their diversity a source of strength and, while embracing international influences, cling firmly to notions of national sovereignty and culture. In contrast to Puritan culture in the United States, which believes that "every contact is a contamination," Mexicans, writes Octavio Paz, "both ancient and modern, believe in communication and fiestas: there is no health without contact."[25] The strength of the Mexican family furnishes an important safeguard against anomie and alienation in a fast-moving, technological, global world. And Mexico's relative youthfulness makes it perhaps an ideal country to

Surprise Scenario:
The Rise of the Governors

One surprise scenario that reflects the new emphases on both pluralism and decentralization is the rapid and discontinuous acquisition of power by Mexico's governors. Although such a trend is already under way, this scenario assumes a greatly accelerated version.

This scenario considers the implications of a massive shift of power from Mexico City to the states in both the short and long term. It is not likely to happen in any fundamental way within the next decade: Mexico City will probably remain the dominant player in national life. But the trend could gather steam during this period.

In contrast to the current, prolonged trend in the same direction, this scenario emerges rapidly and without much warning. A PAN president is elected in 2000, for example, who might fight for—and pass—large portions of a massive devolution program that would transfer important powers to the states. A devastating earthquake could rock the physical and political foundations of the capital, and governors could step into the temporary policy void thus created—and later refuse to step out.

In whatever way it occurs, a major program of decentralization to the state level will have important implications for Mexico's future. So attractive in theory, decentralization could turn out in practice to be a distinctly double-edged sword.

- **Political and economic reform might accelerate in some states** where reformist governors of the left or the right attempt to transfer power from the government to businesses, citizens, and the poor and disenfranchised.

- **The regional divisions in the country, notably the north-south split, might well be exacerbated** as the unifying role of the federal government wanes.

- **Investment strategies for foreign companies would be complicated** by the sudden emergence of differing and conflicting standards, laws, and regulations from state to state.

- **NAFTA might be imperiled** by the actions of several Mexican states seeking to escape its trade requirements.

- **Socioeconomic gaps could widen** if, as seems likely, some states take better advantage than others of the new federalism.

adjust rapidly to the accelerating history and the high-tech climate of the knowledge era.

This strength may partly account for the fact that one finds fairly few references in the Mexican or international press to any psychological cost being paid for globalization, to pleas for new forms of identity and belonging, or to similar signs of social distress at the encounter with the new era. This is not to say that the costs could not rise over time; after all, only a small portion of Mexican society is really a full participant in the knowledge era, and as manifestations of the age seep down into society, large-scale alienation could result. Failure to meet the challenge of institutionalization could make this result especially likely.

All of Mexico's major challenges over the next decade are interlinked. Success at creating virtuous cycles in the economic and institution-building spheres, combined with the country's natural affinity for things global and plural, would come close to guaranteeing the country's health amid the paradoxical demands of the knowledge era. Failure to meet this task could create social alienation where none need exist and magnify the negative dimensions of global-plural interaction over the next decade.

The United States, the recognized engine of Mexico's globalization, will greatly influence the character of that process and the tensions that process generates within Mexico. Careful U.S. attention to Mexican concerns and values as the two countries grow closer economically and culturally is indispensable to a healthy relationship. Amid complaints and accusations about everything from immigration to the environment and drugs, political leaders in Washington often forget their own responsibilities in the bilateral relationship. Mature, generous, respectful U.S. dealings with Mexico in the years ahead will go a long way toward taking the sting out of globalization.

Notes

1. Ernest H. Preeg, *Trade Policy Ahead: Three Tracks and One Question* (Washington, D.C.: Center for Strategic and International Studies, 1995), 13–16.

2. "The Revolution Begins, At Last," and "The Death of Distance," *Economist,* September 30, 1995, 5, 15.

3. United Nations, *World Investment Report: Transnational Corporations, Employment, and the Workforce* (New York: United Nations, 1994), 3–5.

4. Cited in John Naisbitt, *Global Paradox* (New York: William Morrow, 1994), 15.

5. Patrick Glynn, "The Age of Balkanization," *Commentary*, July 1993, 21.

6. "The New America," *U.S. News and World Report*, July 10, 1998, 18–32.

7. François Sabbah, cited in Manuel Castells, *The Rise of the Network Society* (Cambridge: Blackwell, 1996), 339.

8. Samuel Huntington, *The Clash of Civilizations and the Remaking of World Order* (New York: Simon and Schuster, 1996), 129.

9. "Globalization: Is It a Reality?" *Idea Economica*, August 1, 1997; trans. CSIS staff.

10. The information in the issue feature "Global-Local Tensions at the Border" is drawn from Geri Smith and Elizabeth Malkin, "The Border," *Business Week*, May 12, 1997, 64–74.

11. Ronald F. Inglehart, Neil Nevitte, and Miguel Basañez, *The North American Trajectory: Cultural, Economic, and Political Ties among the United States, Canada and Mexico* (New York: Aldine de Gruyter, 1996), 39.

12. Ibid., 1.

13. See, for example, Paul R. Abramson and Ronald Inglehart, *Value Change in Global Perspective* (Ann Arbor: University of Michigan Press, 1995), 124–126.

14. Paula Kephart, "Middle-Class on $10,000 a Year," *American Demographics*, September 1994, 15.

15. OECD, *Economic Surveys: Mexico* (Paris: OECD, 1996), endleaf chart.

16. Robert A. Pastor and Jorge G. Castañeda, *Limits to Friendship: The United States and Mexico* (New York: Vintage Books, 1988), 13, 16, 231, 241.

17. Andres Oppenheimer, *Bordering on Chaos: Guerrillas, Stockbrokers, Politicians, and Mexico's Road to Prosperity* (Boston: Little, Brown and Company, 1996), 64.

18. Ibid., 99–100.

19. Pastor and Castañeda, *Limits to Friendship*, 26, 340-341. Inglehart, Nevitte, and Basañez agree. What the NAFTA partners are moving toward, they write, "is *not* Americanization: the United States is changing like other societies. They are moving toward something new, something that in the long run may provide a global cultural consensus within which

a wide variety of cultures can coexist harmoniously" *(North American Trajectory*, 133).

20. Ruben Martinez, "Mexico's Search for Itself: Cultural Change in Mexico," *The Nation*, April 28, 1997, 22.

21. Andrew Reding, "Facing Political Reality," *Washington Quarterly* 20, no. 4 (Autumn 1997):112–113.

22. Michael Radu, "The Looming Mexican Crisis," *Washington Quarterly*, 20, no. 4 (Autumn 1997): 123.

23. Maarten van Delden, *Carlos Fuentes, Mexico, and Modernity* (Nashville, Tenn.: Vanderbilt University Press, 1998), 4, 7, 9, 197, 201–202.

24. Carlos Fuentes, *A New Time for Mexico* (Berkeley: University of California Press, 1996), 187, 212.

25. Octavio Paz, *The Labyrinth of Solitude and Other Writings,* trans. Lysander Kemp, Yara Milos, and Rachel Phillips Belash (New York: Grove Press, 1985), 24.

5 ■
Trend Five: The Rise of New Authorities

THE TRENDS REVIEWED so far have dramatic implications for a key concept of political and social life: authority. In the knowledge era, the extent and nature of authority in all of its forms are undergoing a profound change. Not only are the social institutions that wield authority affected, but the very character of authority itself. This shift involves something far more complex than a mere "decline of authority," a trend examined for decades. Instead, what is happening today is a transformation of authority and the replacement of its traditional forms by knowledge-era ideas and institutions that exercise great influence over people. Sometimes the new institutions are modified versions of older forms—the partial replacement of monolithic religions, for example, by more diverse and diffuse churches, cults, and self-help gurus—and in other cases, such as the mass media, the form they take is entirely new. But old forms of authority will not give way to new ones overnight, and breaching the gap between the two structures is an immense task.

Phase One: The Decline of Hierarchies

The knowledge era is characterized by a crisis of authority or a decline in the strength of major social institutions. In a fragmented and diversified world, a world of widely available information and greater personal autonomy, a world of relative moral values, ruling groups face unprecedented challenges to their authority. A main reason for this is that the monopolies on information, capital, force, and ideology that were once the source of power for absolute rulers are fading away.

The sociologist Richard Sennett points out that "authority is not a thing. It is an interpretive process which seeks for itself the solidity of a thing."[1] And this interpretive process has begun to move in a new direction. By radically expanding the ability of individuals to participate in it, knowledge renders authorities incapable of preserving a solid front. The weakening of four major forms of social authority—the family, the community (including the nation-state), the church, and tradition—is a measure of the scope of this change. This weakening is not unique to the United States or the West; indeed, the whole world is undergoing a similar kind of social stress.

The well-known decline of the American family, for example, is signaled by dramatically higher rates of divorce and single-parent families. What is not appreciated is that this family decay is global: in many developing countries divorce rates doubled between the 1970s and 1990s. These same pressures conspire to undermine communities, both local and national, around the world. As social mobility and remote forms of interaction have emerged, the strength of civil society has waned. Weaker community institutions contribute to higher levels of crime and corruption, and the next decade could witness a rise in global corruption of epidemic proportions.

Knowledge-era forces tend also to reduce the strength of centralized, hierarchical religions. This does not imply a decline of spirituality or faith—far from it: the next decade could be a time of intensifying religious belief, in part as a reaction to the more alienating trends of our transitional era. But it does suggest that these newer forms of faith will be more plural, decentralized, and flexible. Finally, the force of tradition declines in times of rapid change, when it no longer makes sense—or no longer appears to make sense—to imitate the behavior and values of one's elders.

The most profound effect of the decline of old authorities is social instability. Old, hierarchical forms of authority typically fall away before new ones have fully taken their place, and the result is a weakening of social bonds. An obvious result of this complex dance is the growth of ethnic strife and conflict. Ethnic tension is growing both within societies—in the form of racial tensions in, for example, the United States and Europe—and between them, in the form of ethnically and culturally defined disputes over land or values or trade practices. The decline of the old authorities and the rise of the new makes people intensify their search for identity. This same process, when combined with the uncertainty of the knowledge era, can produce in the individual a dangerous level of alienation.

Phase Two: The Rise of New Authorities

The fate of authority in the knowledge era is not simply one of decline, deterioration, or the permanent victory of alienation. The new authorities rise up to replace the ones that have declined, and in many cases they are more empowering and respectful of freedom than the old (see figure 24).

One form of new authority is the virtual state. Today's basic level of authority, the nation-state, will give way to a less centralized, more flexible, and more adaptable institution. Nation-states will not simply disappear or fall into obsolescence; as virtual states they will share the stage of authority with more actors, accomplishing their tasks with more efficiency and greater frugality. The virtual state's main purpose is to make itself an attractive area for investment, with highly educated populations, modern infrastructures, and moderate tax rates and regulatory schemes.

Peter Drucker suggests that this process of privatization will produce a second and related new form of authority in the knowledge era, which he calls the social sector—or nongovernmental organizations performing services previously held to be government responsibilities. Recent numbers do indeed show the dramatic growth of the social sector: not only does the United States alone boast almost a million and a half nonprofit groups; the economic activity of these groups, at roughly 7 percent of U.S. GNP, exceeds the GNP of all but seven nations in the world.

A concept that functions as a sort of social authority in the knowledge era is a novel set of dominant business strategies, perhaps best reflected in Gary Hamel's notion of "strategy as revolution." The idea is that, in an era of "hypercompetition" and rapid product turnover, trying to preserve existing market share without innovation is disastrous and pursuing "incremental improvements while rivals reinvent the industry is like fiddling while Rome burns."[2] Never before

> **Figure 24**
> **Characteristics of Knowledge-Era Authorities**
>
> - In their *organization* they will be decentralized, small, and flexible—most often specialized, single-issue groups. In an age of micromarketing and diversity, few broad-based institutions will succeed.
>
> - In many cases their *physical structure* will be virtual instead of concrete; many will consist of far-flung, pluralistic conglomerations working together.
>
> - Their approach to *power* will not be coercive; they will seek influence rather than control or outright power. These new institutions will be centers of information and knowledge competing for allegiance rather than rigid authorities as we have known them.
>
> - Their *method of acquiring influence* will be through performance, competence, and effectiveness rather than through brute force or tradition.

"has the world been more hospitable to industry revolutionaries and more hostile to industry incumbents." The knowledge era demands an "*innovation-rich* economy," writes former Citibank president Walter Wriston. "Nations that wish to flourish . . . will have to foster a climate of innovation."[3]

The principles of new business strategies lead directly to a new form of business authority: new management styles.

Modern management theories aim to place more and more control in the hands of workers at the expense of middle management. Knowledge-era corporate leaders have decentralized decisionmaking and have empowered their employees more than at any time in the modern era.

Direct democracy constitutes the political expression of new forms of authority in the knowledge era. The combination of television, telephone, and computer lines that is developing under the rubric of "the information superhighway" is changing the way that Americans participate in politics. Public opinion polling, referenda, ballot initiatives—all someday conducted via voting boxes attached to televisions—are bringing politics closer to the people.

The character of businesses will also change in the knowledge era as they accept new roles beyond mere profit making. "Ten years from now, I am firmly convinced," writes James Moore, "business leaders will be actively and daily addressing social and environmental issues."[4] The reasons are not altruistic: they include the corporate need for a well-trained workforce; competition to attract mobile workers; efforts to increase retention and productivity; and concerns for public image and trust. Companies that express a sense of broader social responsibilities will reap the rewards, both internally and externally.

Finally, the ultimate authority in the knowledge era is the most decentralized of all: the individual human being. Our era empowers human beings with more freedom, choice, and opportunity than at any other time in human history. This new age calls for self-sufficient, self-motivated, self-navigating people—individuals who express the new degrees of social and personal responsibility that are so necessary in an era of rapid change.

Applying the Trends to Mexico: Renewing Social Order

The issues raised by the transformation of authority point toward what may well be the overriding challenge for Mexico in the coming decade: solidifying the rule of law and strengthening the social and political institutions that underwrite it. Crime, corruption, and the invasion of drugs are carcinogens in any society, but they are particularly deadly for a developing nation struggling through domestic and international transitions in political and economic life. It does not make Mexico's task any easier that its own situation calls for a reconstruction of social institutions at precisely the moment that a global transition is requiring a broader and more fundamental version of the same thing of all nations. The emergence of the knowledge era magnifies the degree and pace of change that developing nations such as Mexico must undergo in the coming decade. In the blink of history's eye, Mexico must progress, not merely to industrialism, but to postindustrialism; not merely to modernism, but to postmodernism; not merely to materialist values, but to postmaterialist ones.

At first glance Mexico would not seem to be well-equipped to leapfrog historical eras. In part this is true because, as has often been said, Mexico has traditionally been a "country of men, not institutions." Top political leaders, especially the president, often made autocratic policy decisions unencumbered by the checks and balances of a democratic political system. Loyalty in Mexican politics was to individuals first and institutions second.

> The challenge that Mexico faces over the next decade is nothing less than the creation of a full-fledged civil society from a situation in which the state—and, in fact, certain individuals within the state—have dominated the social scene.

Here we see an especially stark contrast between virtuous and vicious cycles: virtuous cycles involving the gradual strengthening of institutions, and vicious ones their erosion in the face of increasing instability. These institutions are now emerging, but perhaps not quickly enough. The next decade will reveal whether the emerging trends will interrupt that construction of a stronger civic society and a democratic political system. Sidney Weintraub has pointed out that President Zedillo has been "compared to Mikhail Gorbachev for dismantling the old Mexican political system and leaving uncertainty in its place. This is the potential downside of the political opening, that it might be accompanied by turmoil and instability."[5]

The Degeneration of Old Authorities

At the base of the profound transformation of authority under way in Mexican society is the erosion of the monolithic, corporatist PRI and the shift to a more diversified civil society. The growth of a more competitive democratic system is a political earthquake that has shaken the foundations of Mexican society, weakening dozens of secondary institutions that relied on the PRI for their authority and opening the way for hundreds of other groups and organizations—some benign, some selfish, some brutally violent—to seize more influential social roles.

This is not to suggest that the PRI has declined beyond the point of recovery. It has begun to experiment with open primaries, a trend that may help it bring more centrist, reform-oriented candidates into general elections. In a March 1998 gubernatorial primary, for example, an old-guard PRI candidate who apparently agreed to the runoff as a formality lost to a change-oriented, pro-business PRIista. The PRI could begin to transform itself into a more responsive party offering a middle way between the laissez-faire PAN and the statist PRD. In general, though, the knowledge era tends to disempower politics and political parties in favor of other social actors. This process is likely to continue and even accelerate in Mexico whether or not the PRI makes a comeback.

Another longer-term global transition is one that outstrips political parties altogether through the influence of repersonalized politics, electronic democracy, and decentralized decisionmaking. This trend so far has limited relevance for Mexico, which must pass through the stage of modern democracy before it arrives at its postmodern version. Yet the inevitable transformation of what we call democracy makes the country's political transition even more urgent. The political parties that Mexico is struggling to create—and which are so critical to a stable polity—are already living on borrowed time. The country faces the unenviable task of solidifying its democratic transition before the tidal wave of knowledge-era hyperdemocracy washes away all of the familiar political landmarks.

This shift reflects a "deep-rooted shift in the nature of mass orientations toward government" in Mexico (and around the world), as Inglehart, Nevitte, and Basañez explain:

> The authority of governments to tell their people what to do is in gradual but long-term decline. Conversely, the public is becoming increasingly adept at telling governments what to do—and increasingly likely to intervene directly in political decisionmaking.

The political transformation is in turn part of the broader trend toward greater autonomy, independence, and empowerment—the "declining acceptance of the authority of hierarchical institutions, both political and nonpolitical." The percentage of Mexicans expressing support in the world values survey for "autonomy over obedience in child-rearing values," for example, jumped from 10 percent in 1981 to 32 percent in 1990. During the same period the level of support for "greater respect for authority" declined slightly, from 67 to 65 percent.[6]

Apart from the federal government, then, we find other authorities besieged as well. Although the emphasis on family duty remains higher in Mexico than in most industrialized nations—furnishing the country with a certain advantage in dealing with specific new trends—that emphasis is receding. Poll results from 1981 to 1990 point to a "sizable *decline* in emphasis on family values," with the percentage of Mexican respondents to the world values survey ranking high on a "family duty scale" falling from 82 to 70 percent.[7] Similarly, in attitudes toward religion the authority of traditional church institutions is on the wane. Between 1981 and 1990, the percentage of world values survey respondents classifying themselves as very religious fell from 48 percent to 40 and the proportion attending church at least once a month dropped from 75 percent to 63 percent. In line with the global trend, however, what is at work is not a decline of spirituality per se—in the same period, the number of Mexicans who said they "'often' think about the meaning and purpose of life" actually rose from 32 to 40 percent—but a challenge to hierarchical institutions. "As long as most churches base their appeal on the need for absolute, predictable rules," Inglehart, Nevitte, and Basañez conclude, "their decline is likely to continue."[8]

Various forms of community also seem to be fraying. Urban migration and the collapse of many agrarian economies have undermined hundreds of small villages. Urbanization and social mobility inherently weaken the sense of community. The nation-state itself may also be weakening, both because of growing regionalism and because of the thorough "denationalization" of life. As is true globally, however, the state will remain fairly healthy over the next decade: the time period under consideration will not see the end of the nation-state, but the end of statism, the dominant role of the state in many societies of the world. And in fact this trend is accompanied by the need to build a stronger nation-state in various ways—especially, more robust institutions of democratic governance—amid a worldwide move away from state power. This is far from being the only paradoxical task facing Mexico over the next 10 years, but it may be the most important.

Transitional Risks: Symptoms of Social Instability

As Mexico undergoes a social, political, and economic transition from one kind of authority structure to another—a transition hastened and magnified by a parallel global shift of the same kind—its leaders will be hard-pressed to preserve social order and the rule of law. Already a number of worrisome trends have emerged that call into question the country's ability to make this transition smoothly.

Political and Economic Corruption

This is a classic problem in Mexico, as in virtually every nondemocratic system. There has been a prevailing assumption that corruption was the exclusive product of a PRI-dominated government and will therefore dissipate once political freedom and transparency in government strip away the screens behind which corrupt politicians hide. But the experience of other reforming states suggests that the worst may be yet to come: corruption took root in Russia, Eastern Europe, and elsewhere in the early stages of reform, after the yoke of repression was thrown off but before new democratic institutions were strong enough to enforce the laws. The growing influence of narcotraffickers, massive amounts of money made in informal and illegal sectors of the economy, and dubious ties among businesses, organized crime, police, and paramilitary organizations have created similar versions of feudal-style rule in some areas of Mexico, where corruption is the norm rather than the exception.

Mexico, of course, has some advantages that Russia does not, such as the vitality of its reformist governments and the more established role of independent social forces such as business, the church, and nongovernmental organizations. If the evolution of Mexico's new democratic institutions lags, however, criminals, businesspeople, government officials, and other social groups may conclude that legitimacy is unattainable and the only realistic alternative is to seek personal gain. Average Mexicans, meanwhile, will decide that their cynical view of government and politicians is more justified than ever, further undermining public confidence in the problem-solving authority of society. All of this suggests that the gap between public (and international) expectations for Mexico's nascent democracy and the practices of those accustomed to working in, and benefiting from, the old system will only grow wider.

Crime

As the influence of social institutions declines, the incidence of crime frequently rises, making it a convenient indicator of transformations in structures of authority. Mexico certainly reflects this trend. In 1996 more than 250,000 crimes were reported in Mexico City, including 13 car thefts an hour and three murders a day. In 1997 more than 1,300 crimes were directed at tourists. Reported crimes in the city have jumped from 350 per day in 1993 to more than 700 a day in 1997—and some estimates suggest that 90 percent of all crime in the capital goes unreported. Also in 1997, there were more than a million muggings, and in the 18 months preceding January 1998 there were 3,000 kidnappings of Mexicans for ransom.[9]

Things have gotten so bad in Mexico City that one brazen armed band stole a van and $50,000 worth of camera equipment in April 1998 from a CNN television crew standing 50 feet from the Mexican foreign ministry, surrounded at the time by dozens of Mexican police, and where U.S. drug czar Barry McCaffrey was attending a conference on drug smuggling. Mexico's crime rate has multiplied faster in the last 4 years than in the previous 60.[10] Dozens of city taxis, some painted to resemble the official "Sitio" cabs, respond to intercepted calls and participate in kidnapping and robbery rings, collecting passengers only to deliver them into the waiting hands of criminals.[11]

The Inter-American Development Bank has put a figure on one economic result of the region's crime wave: Latin America as a whole, the bank estimates, loses $168 billion a year in development because of crime and violence, equivalent to 14 percent of regional GDP.[12] No wonder, then, that President Zedillo remarked in his September 1998 state of the nation address, "In all honesty, we must admit that where public safety is concerned, those of us in all three branches of government . . . have failed out citizens."[13]

Criminal activity takes on an especially threatening guise in transitional periods because it can reflect not only the activities of a few lawbreakers, but the general collapse of respect for social norms. Recent survey evidence reinforces this trend: the percentage of Mexicans saying it is sometimes permissible to buy stolen goods, drive a stolen car, accept a bribe, or threaten workers who strike rose from 32 percent in 1981 to 55 percent in 1990.[14] A thorough collapse of social order becomes a real possibility when exploding levels of crime and corruption convince the majority of a population that the social contract no longer functions. Criminal activity is then the norm, social order the exception. Inasmuch as this development depends as much on perceptions as on actual deeds, it is especially worrisome that sensationalistic media have worked to make Mexico's crime problem appear even worse than it is by covering grisly crime stories in detail every day.

Considered objectively, social violence is not out of control in Mexico as it is in some African nations. The level of homicides was not quite double that of the United States, less than that of Brazil, and orders of magnitude below that of the region's model of a criminal society, Colombia. Mexico's homicide rate, moreover, may actually have declined slightly since the late 1970s.[15] Any claims of a leap to the collapse of all social order remain an exaggeration—but the trends are running in precisely that direction, and current levels of crime are, if not chaotic, nonetheless unacceptable. To build a stable foundation for achieving other social, economic, and political goals, Mexico must overcome its problem of social violence.

Drug Trafficking

Arguably no single trend poses a greater risk to structures of authority than narcotrafficking. One estimate suggests that 70 percent of all marijuana and cocaine arriving in the United States originates in or transits through Mexico, with $30 billion in drug money laundered near the border each year.[16] Another study has found that more than seven tons of cocaine, marijuana, and heroin cross the U.S.-Mexican border every day.[17] Anecdotal evidence from northern Mexico suggests that the problem is worsening, that Mexican drug lords have gained strength, and that U.S., Mexican, and other Latin American narcotraffickers are forging strategic alliances stretching throughout the hemisphere and beyond.

Because of their insidious character, these phenomena have unmatched potential to destabilize Mexican society. Drug money is infiltrating every Mexican institution, from the police to the courts to the military and even, some reports now suggest, to Mexico's Congress. A recent U.S. law enforcement operation also suggests that Mexican banks may be more involved in laundering drug money than had been assumed; Washington indicted officials from three of Mexico's largest banks and believes that 12 of the biggest 19 banks are involved with drug money.[18] At the end of this road lies the Colombianization of Mexico, where narcotrafficking and its influence have spread throughout the country like a cancer. In such a scenario Mexico would be a democracy in name only, social violence would be widespread, and the country's economic fortunes would plummet as foreign investment left for safer harbors. Controlling the drug business is the race against time par excellence, the single most urgent aspect of the broader challenge of dampening corruption and building an effective and stable civil society.

Mexico's drug industry also looms as a serious threat to the long-term health of U.S.-Mexican relations. Recent reports suggest that Mexican drug cartels are increasingly prominent in the U.S. market—becoming, for example, the second-largest source of heroin used in the United States.[19] But Mexico often perceives U.S. counter-drug operations as implicit or explicit violations of its sovereignty—a view that, transmitted through the U.S. State Department, may have constrained those operations. "American drug fighters in the front line," the *Economist* reported in May 1998, "often complain that their dangerous work is made irrelevant because their government fails to act as energetically against Mexico's mobs as it has against Colombian ones."[20] These various factors—rising drug smuggling from Mexico, lagging U.S. enforcement, anger and embarrassment in Mexico in response to U.S. operations that do take place—are on a collision course, and could easily produce a new wave of resentment between the two countries.

Insurgent Movements

A by-product of a number of other social ills, from inequity to corruption, are the lingering insurgent movements, mostly in the south

Surprise Scenario:
Explosion in Narcotrafficking

One of the most serious threats to the stability and peace of Mexican society is the growing influence of narcotraffickers. Because this trend is already well established, this surprise scenario assumes a new kind of drug trade of vaster magnitude and potentially more detrimental effect.

This scenario considers the implications of a sudden, dramatic upsurge in drug-related violence and corruption centered in Mexico City and areas around the border with the United States.

This growing reach of narcotrafficking can be measured in many ways, from the number of gang-related violent deaths, to the discovery of efforts by drug kingpins to buy off members of the executive and legislative branches, to evidence of a greater volume of drugs crossing the U.S. border. Its implications could include the following signs of the "Colombianization" of Mexican society:

- **The weakening of Mexico's embryonic democracy** as public policy increasingly seems to serve the drug barons rather than the people, leading to mounting popular disaffection with elected officials.

- **The discrediting of the government's economic liberalization program** as the government is seen as protecting the interests of criminal groups.

- **Rising social violence** in all forms, from gang-related drug deaths to common crime.

- **Accelerated illegal immigration** into the United States as violence grows, resulting in rising U.S.-Mexican tensions—tensions also stemming from the perception that Mexico is losing its "war on drugs."

- **Plummeting foreign direct investment** as international businesses seek a more stable climate for their capital. Eventually economic growth stalls, unemployment rises, and the government's economic reform effort sustains another mortal blow. Tourism could also decline precipitously, costing Mexico billions more.

- **Mexico's democracy stillborn** as the influence of the drug lords represses voices of dissent throughout the society.

and southeastern parts of the country. The Zapatista National Liberation Army burst onto the national scene in 1994 with a small series of attacks in Chiapas, demanding "democracy, land, food, housing and justice." In June 1996 a second insurgent movement, the Ejército Revolucionario Popular (ERP), established its presence. Although the actual damage the groups have wrought to property and lives is limited, their broader impact on perceptions is substantial—especially abroad, where focus is on the ongoing Chiapas conflict. If social conditions worsen over the next decade, these movements could destabilize Mexico by propagating the impression of a country on the brink of collapse.

Even though the number of weapon-carrying members remains fairly small, these groups cast into doubt the government's ability to solve the country's problems. The government's shortcomings are especially problematic for a regime that considers itself democratic, representative, and reformist. If it cannot represent the interests of the rebels and their sympathizers, some argue, the government cannot claim to be truly inclusive; if it cannot address the sources of their grievances, it cannot claim to be a healing force. With the simple application of brute force, Mexico's military could likely defeat the major insurgent movements in a matter of days, but that would not be in keeping with the country's new democratic tradition and its emphasis on negotiated solutions to social disputes. And so contrary to the unstated assumption of some observers, these tensions will be all the more pressing as reform proceeds, because they raise the fundamental question of why a democratic government is unable to resolve conflicts within its midst.

The Rise of New Authorities

At the same time, new forms of social authority are on the rise in Mexico, as they are globally, and are filling the space vacated by those on the decline. A host of institutions that once played passive roles as segments of the PRI-dominated system are now finding their voices. The rapid emergence of the kinds of institutions described below would lay the groundwork for a virtuous cycle in which stronger authorities make headway on social problems, public cynicism eases, and economic and social progress accelerates. These new authorities must gain power rapidly to prevent a more complete collapse of social order.

The new authorities in Mexico are both within government and outside and have both governmental and nongovernmental components.

Government Institutions

Mexico urgently needs to construct institutions within the government that will make the democratic transition irreversible and will ensure the permanence of social order. This is somewhat different than the situation of highly industrialized nations, where well-entrenched democratic institutions are increasingly sharing authority with nongovernmental organizations. Mexico thus confronts a double challenge: that of building an effective democratic structure while nurturing its own version of the global trend toward nongovernmental activism.

Probably the most important rising governmental authority is the Congress, a body that has acquired real authority at the price of reduced influence for the PRI. A more influential legislature could begin to introduce into Mexican politics the sorts of checks and balances that have been conspicuously absent in the past. To exercise its newfound power, the Congress will need larger staffs, more time to consider legislation, and bigger institutional budgets; steps to achieve these gains have already been undertaken. It will have to establish the principle of reelection rather than limiting members to one term, which constrains accountability. Above all, its newly elected members must learn the art of compromise, which is so essential to democracy. This skill seemed in short supply in the wake of the 1997 elections, which broke the PRI's majority and led to months of deadlock.

A second governmental authority of growing importance is the PAN, a political party with the potential to reshape Mexican politics. Perhaps more easily than the PRD, which is dominated by Càrdenas and which many view as favoring old-style statist solutions to social ills, the PAN could emerge as a nationwide force for reform and change. Such an outcome is not guaranteed; some PAN governors have flexed their muscles in support of a religious and free-market orthodoxy that is as extreme as any of the leftist dogmas that some believe still dominate the PRD. But in other places PAN officials have proved to be some of the country's most ardent supporters of innovation and bold reformism.

Acknowledging the need for economic decisionmaking to be institutionalized, efforts are already under way to give more clout to a third governmental authority, the head of the central bank. A stronger central bank could be the most important new authority in Mexican economics over the next decade, and a central bank directorship wielding the kind of influence enjoyed by Alan Greenspan would, if the post were similarly nonpolitical, help rein in the nearly unlimited power of the presidency.

Bold and forward-thinking mayors and governors constitute the fourth—and in the long run perhaps the most important—rising governmental authority. Important new policies are springing up at the state or local level, often encouraged by governors. State and local governments will have to become active in promoting small and medium-sized business. This is an immense change from the way of doing business in the past, and it reflects the decentralized character of the knowledge era.

Decentralization of power in Mexico may edge the country closer to the ideal of local governance that Carlos Fuentes has so eloquently advocated.

Traditions of self-government" in Mexico are not as weak as commonly assumed, Fuentes observes. "Our town halls, whenever given a chance, have proved that Mexicans can rule themselves," and they could foster the kind of "imaginative, decentralized, self-governing" movements so critical to the nation's economic future.[21] This dream, seemingly quixotic during the decades of highly centralized PRI rule, does not look so utopian in the context of the knowledge era, and it could provide a rallying vision for one or more political parties. Empowering local governments will be a major challenge in a country where the federal government collects 99 percent of the taxes;[22] if it took place in an environment of instability, moreover, decentralization could rapidly become a dangerous sort of fragmentation. But the global trend in this direction is clear enough, and Fuentes and others have merely emphasized that Mexico has political and social traditions amenable to local governance.

A somewhat more sinister form of emerging governmental authority is the military. After decades of strict obedience to civilian powers, the military has recently gained strength as a social actor. The "demilitarization of Mexico" in the twentieth century, Enrique Krauze reminds us, "was a phenomenon as admirable as it was mysterious, especially when contrasted with the military background of Mexican history."[23] That background may now be returning to view as the government calls on the military to play a broader role in society, from fighting drug trafficking to combating insurgent movements and taking charge of police duties. Burgeoning paramilitary groups complement the role of the formal military. In addition to its other tasks of institutionalization, then, Mexico must also reinculcate a culture of loyalty and democratic accountability in its military—an institution that bears close supervision in the coming decade.

Nongovernmental Authorities: The Social Sector

Nongovernmental organizations and citizens groups, some tracing their origins to spontaneous community activism after the massive 1985 earthquake, are contributing to "an increasingly vigorous civic society" that has begun to "challenge the government on virtually all fronts." The number of nongovernmental organizations has grown from a few hundred in the 1980s to perhaps 1,300 in the mid-1990s.[24]

Charitable organizations have also blossomed. Most of them have emerged recently; the head of one Mexican nonprofit has estimated that two-thirds of the philanthropic groups in the country are less than 30 years old. His group has some 4,300 charitable groups in its official directory, but he estimates that the total may run to 20,000 or more.[25] Neighborhood groups, such as crime watches, seem also to be on the rise.

The emergence of a fuller civil society in Mexico goes hand in hand with the country's democratic reforms, and the two trends are mutually supportive. Until recently the state dominated social space in Mexico; however, democracy and economic liberalization are opening the way for other groups to take up important roles. These groups in turn assume some of the burdens—fighting poverty, protecting the environment, redistributing wealth, providing police functions, and so on—formerly assumed to be the unique provenance of government. They may embody Mexico's best opportunity to renew public faith in social institutions: in contrast to their attitudes about government, the proportion of Mexicans expressing confidence in nongovernmental institutions actually rose slightly between 1981 and 1990, an astonishing development in a country where cynicism rules public perceptions.

Carlos Fuentes has recognized the critical role that the third, or social, sector must play in Mexico's progress. "Small, original, innovating," he has written, "the organizations of the third sector are helping to set the agenda for the twenty-first century throughout the world. They give power back to the people. They can help bridge the chasm between the two Mexicos." In particular, Fuentes sees the social sector as an indispensable source of balance between liberal economics and social justice, between the "market economy [and] social commitments"—a balance that, if maintained, will create a "virtuous cycle" of social progress.[26]

Religion constitutes a second key nongovernmental authority in Mexico. The Catholic Church occupies a place of immense importance—and of controversy, with close government-clerical partnerships having, in the view of some, contributed to the country's authoritarianism. Even in an era of declining religiosity, the influence of the church may be on the rise: the *Economist* recently noted that, "like a giant waking from a long sleep, Mexico's Catholic church is beginning to stir." The Mexican archbishop Noberto Rivera Carrera was quoted as telling an audience of 30,000 in a Mexico City bullring that the country is in "a state of economic, political, social, and religious crisis."

This new activism is the product in part of the electoral defeat of the PRI, which has encouraged many groups to speak out more loudly. With other social authorities such as the government and the military under attack, Mexicans hope religious leaders and institutions

Issue Feature:
Evangelicals in Mexico

In recent years, Evangelical Protestantism seemed to spread like wildfire throughout Mexico. It is now clear that the Evangelical movement has its limits, though it will remain a potent force.

The Evangelical movement is almost exclusively the province of poor Mexicans, frustrated with their lot in life and looking for new forms of belonging. From less than a million in 1970, the Evangelical population reached 4 million in 1990 and 6 million by 1996, growing at a rate five times faster than Catholicism. If the Evangelical churches could keep all of their converts, they would become the leading religion in Mexico by the year 2006.

This would be a shocking turnabout for a nation so long known for its staunch Catholicism and a change that would have powerful implications for Mexican culture, politics, and society. Look a little closer, though, and it becomes obvious that Protestantism is not about to leapfrog the Catholic Church on Mexico's spiritual roster.

At about 6 percent of the population, Mexico's Protestants do not begin to compare in influence to those in Chile (28 percent) or Brazil (22 percent). And the fact is that Evangelical churches are losing converts almost as fast as they gain them: for whatever reason—perhaps because many of these churches are as easy to leave as they are to join, or perhaps because the requirements of the faith are too strict—the majority of Mexican Evangelicals abandon their faith as adults or within several years after first converting. Thus fully 43 percent of those raised as Evangelicals drop out as adults, and almost 70 percent of those converted in the 1980s had abandoned the church by the end of that decade.

While Evangelical Protestantism is thriving in Mexico, then, and the movement bears close watching, **talk of a "Protestant Mexico" in the early twenty-first century seems premature.**[29] And in the long run, as this chapter has argued, the more fundamental spiritual trend looks past hierarchically organized religious institutions altogether.

Issue Feature:
Knowledge-Era Business Strategy in Mexico

Cultural barriers to success in business extend to the realm of business management and strategy, the area in which cutting-edge, knowledge-era concepts of social organization are most pervasive. Queen's University professor of management and organizational behavior Shawna O'Grady assessed a number of cultural barriers in a 1995 survey of executives in Mexico.

Perhaps the attitude most at odds with knowledge-era concepts is the emphasis on hierarchy. "Relations between superiors and subordinates in Mexico are dictated by hierarchy," O'Grady found. "Centralized decision-making is the norm, and Mexican employees are reluctant to take on any responsibility at work." As a result, "title and position are usually sufficient to enforce authority"—precisely the opposite of knowledge-era businesses. These trends are reinforced by Mexico's educational system, which "rewards rote learning and deference to authority."

Another barrier to modern business practice is a lack of trust: "the family is of utmost importance" and loyalty at work is directed only to one's supervisor. As a result, a number of companies have had trouble using work teams. Another problem is the famous "*mañana* syndrome"; executives told her that "getting things done quickly or even on time in Mexico was next to impossible."[30]

Yet there is some evidence that these attitudes are changing. The Covey Leadership Center has maintained an office in Mexico for 12 years to help bring concepts like teams and empowerment to Mexican companies. And one management consultant argues that the best and most modern Mexican companies "believe in and use a participative management style, with teamwork as its central core."[31] Still, the challenge is not a small one—the Covey Center's director defines it as nothing less that a "top-to-bottom overhaul of the Mexican work style."[32]

One grossly false stereotype is that Mexicans do not work hard; O'Grady replies that they work extremely hard and that their perceived lack of motivation should be "attributed to the belief that they have little control over their lives, which in turn discourages effort and initiative."[33] **As the workplace changes, so will the incentive structure—and behavior.**

might help fill the void.²⁷ Other developments, including constitutional reforms and a more active Vatican representative, have also boosted the church's influence.

The notion that business—a third nongovernmental authority of growing importance—should play a constructive social role is in its infancy, but seems to be developing. An example of this is in the areas of environmental protection. Larger businesses are beginning to realize that improved environmental practices yield immense public relations and economic benefits. "Many companies plying the European and U.S. markets with their goods benefit from a greener marketing image," notes reporter Jeff Wright. "As a result, a lot of industries are now taking steps toward" internationally recognized environmental certifications.²⁸

New business strategies are also slowly spreading, and these will nudge Mexican business practices toward greater participation and empowerment. The participative, nonhierarchical, empowering corporate management and strategic models now dominant in the industrial world are being adopted by Mexican companies and, even more intensively, by multinational companies operating in Mexico. As this happens Mexican business, like knowledge-era businesses throughout the world, will set the standard for the participatory and decentralizing trends of the age. As the issue feature "Knowledge-Era Business Strategy" notes, there are significant cultural barriers to the adoption of techniques that so boldly undermine traditional forms of social organization. But these barriers are increasingly surmounted as businesses and their employees search for more effective and more rewarding ways to run the office.

Survey results furnish interesting, and somewhat contradictory, results on this issue. The proportion of Mexicans favoring employee participation in business management remains much higher than in the United States, suggesting an affinity with the principles of knowledge-era business. Yet that proportion has actually been declining in recent years. But the paradox has a straightforward explanation: while the legacy of revolutionary ideas impels Mexicans to favor participatory institutions, the "dismal performance of Mexican state-owned industries" that have institutionalized these ideas lends support to "the idea of turning authority over to independent ownership" as "a healthy corrective to slow strangulation by an over-centralized state."³⁴

The same tendency underlies Mexicans' opinions about whether people should "follow instructions" at work: while the number of people agreeing with this sentiment is declining in the industrialized world, reflecting the knowledge-era tendency to challenge authority, the percentage is rising in Mexico because Mexicans appreciate the need to improve the professionalism of business.

Dozens of Mexican companies are now absorbing the lessons of knowledge-era management strategy. One example is PIPSA, a paper manufacturer that once held a monopoly on newsprint production. Liberalization brought competition and, ultimately, privatization to this state-run firm, and it has responded by implementing state-of-the-art management techniques. To promote creativity, for example, participants in one meeting on corporate strategy were asked to explain their ideas by singing songs about them. CEO René Villareal has grouped most of his 2,000 employees into 100 "learning cells" of 8 to 40 people—a version of the concept of work teams. Stressing the importance of nurturing a learning environment, Villareal has instructed the teams to focus on the development of productive knowledge. The "only way for us to compete is with knowledge," Villareal says of his company's new need to compete against giant conglomerates. "The old paradigm of Mexico as a place for cheap labor is no longer true: our advantage is *productive* labor."³⁵

Octavio Paz put the challenge this way:

> We must break up the existing monopolies—whether of the state, of parties, or of private capitalism—and discover forms, new and truly effective forms, of democratic and popular control over political and economic power and over the information media and education. A plural society, without majorities or minorities: not all of us are happy in my political utopia, but at least all of us are responsible.³⁶

In its focus on highly educated human resources and continual retraining, PIPSA is in a distinct minority of companies. But CEO Villareal has it exactly right: if Mexico is to catapult itself into the knowledge era, it must shed the image (and reality) of a typical low-wage, export-oriented developing nation, and modern business strategies can help. By adopting them Mexican firms will begin slowly to change the mindsets of their employees and train them for the social patterns of the knowledge era.

Notes

1. Richard Sennett, *Authority* (New York: W. W. Norton, 1980), 19.

2. Gary Hamel, "Strategy as Revolution," *Harvard Business Review* 74, no. 4 (1996): 69-71.

3. Walter Wriston, *The Twilight of Sovereignty* (New York: Scribner's, 1992), 127.

4. James F. Moore, *The Death of Competition: Leadership and Strategy in the Age of Business Ecosystems* (New York: HarperBusiness, 1996), 272-273.

5. Sidney Weintraub, "The Complex Situation That Is Mexico," *Washington Quarterly* 20, no. 4 (Autumn 1997):96.

6. Ronald F. Inglehart, Neil Nevitte, and Miguel Basañez, *The North American Trajectory: Cultural, Economic, and Political Ties among the United States, Canada and Mexico* (New York: Aldine de Gruyter, 1996), 104, 105–106, 69-72.

7. Ibid., 73-74.

8. Ibid., 77-81. See also Ronald Inglehart, *Modernization and Postmodernization* (Princeton, N.J.: Princeton University Press, 1997), 376–377.

9. Susan Ferriss, "Crime in Mexico Prompts Tourists, Foreign Residents to Take Special Precautions," Cox News Service, April 23, 1998, wire report; Maria Puente, "Safety of Travel to Mexico in Question," Gannett News Service, April 22, 1998, wire report.

10. Brook Larmer, "Living in Fear," *Newsweek*, April 20, 1998, 17.

11. John Ward Anderson, "Crime Wave Complicates Mexico City Mayor's Promise to Curb Lawlessness," *Washington Post*, December 23, 1997, p. A13.

12. Larmer, "Living in Fear."

13. Cited in *Washington Post*, September 2, 1998, p. A26.

14. Inglehart, Nevitte, and Basañez, *North American Trajectory*, 76.

15. Shahid Javed Burki and Guillermo E. Perry, *The Long March: A Reform Agenda for Latin America and the Caribbean in the Next Decade* (Washington, D.C.: World Bank, 1997), 66.

16. Robert D. Kaplan, "History Moving North," *Atlantic*, February 1997, 22.

17. John Ward Anderson, "Letter to the Editor: Mexican Standoff," *Foreign Policy* 110 (Spring 1998): 192.

18. Douglas Farah, "Mexican Banks Laundered Drug Money, U.S. Charges," *Washington Post*, May 19, 1998, p. A1.

19. Molly Moore and Douglas Farah, "Mexicans Build U.S. Heroin Market," *Washington Post*, June 2, 1998, p. A1.

20. "Yankee Drug-Busters Head South," *Economist*, May 23, 1998, p. 31.

21. Carlos Fuentes, *A New Time for Mexico* (Berkeley: University of California Press, 1996), 82-83.

22. OECD, *Environmental Performance Review: Mexico* (Paris: OECD, 1998), 43.

23. Enrique Krauze, *Mexico: Biography of Power*, trans. Hank Heifetz (New York: HarperCollins, 1997), 509.

24. Andres Oppenheimer, *Bordering on Chaos: Guerrillas, Stockbrokers, Politicians, and Mexico's Road to Prosperity* (Boston: Little, Brown and Company, 1996), 169.

25. Jorge Villalobos, presentation to World Bank seminar "Culture in Latin America," Washington, D.C., February 24, 1998.

26. Fuentes, *New Time for Mexico*, xii-xiii, 137.

27. "Mexico Politics: The Church Finds Its Voice," *Economist*, December 8, 1997.

28. Jeff Wright, "Cleanup Time," *Business Mexico*, June 1997, 52.

29. Statistics in the issue feature "Evangelicals in Mexico" come from Kurt Bowen, *Evangelism and Apostasy: The Evolution and Impact of Evangelicals in Modern Mexico* (Montreal: McGill-Queen's University Press, 1996), 218–228.

30. All quotes from Shawna O'Grady, "Doing Business in Mexico: The Human Resource Challenges," *Business Quarterly*, Autumn 1995, 44–49.

31. Eva Kras, "Doing Business in Mexico," comment on the Shawna O'Grady essay, *Business Quarterly*, Winter 1995, 19.

32. Olga Morales, "The Flip Side," *Business Mexico*, July 1997, 32–33.

33. O'Grady, "Doing Business."

34. Inglehart, Nevitte, and Basañez, *North American Trajectory*, 113.

35. Eric Matson, "You Can Teach This Old Company New Tricks," *Fast Company,* October-November 1997, 44–46.

36. Octavio Paz, *The Labyrinth of Solitude and Other Writings,* trans. Lysander Kemp, Yara Milos, and Rachel Phillips Belash (New York: Grove Press, 1985), 282–283.

6 ∎
Trend Six: A Test of Human Psychology

IT IS CLEAR THAT THE ADVENT OF THE KNOWLEDGE ERA, with its associated social and economic transformations, will put individuals under immense strain. Coping with change is never easy; coping with the rapid and comprehensive changes under way today could turn out to be one of the hardest tests ever put to the human race. The character of that test will determine its social and personal implications for human psychology and, in turn, the requirements for meeting it successfully.

Anxiety and the Psychological Challenge

"We have reached a moment in history," argues self-esteem guru Nathaniel Branden, "when self-esteem, which has always been a supremely important psychological need, has become an urgent economic need." The new global economy is "characterized by rapid change, accelerating scientific and technological breakthroughs, and an unprecedented level of competitiveness." While everyone in the business world understands that this fact magnifies the importance of education, Branden writes, what is not so well understood is that the new pressures "also create new demands on our psychological resources," asking for "a greater capacity for innovation, self-management, personal responsibility, and self-direction."[1]

As citizens of the knowledge era, we are expected to understand our own career and life choices well enough to make them intelligently. We are expected to master dozens of kinds of advanced technology, from computers to automobiles to videotape recorders. We have to manage a lifelong process of education in support of our careers (or interests), of its substance as well as its finance. We must pay our bills and complete complicated tax forms and manage a portfolio of insurance, retirement savings, and other investments. We must provide for our health care, wending our way through a maze of complicated insurance options and care restrictions and regulations.

The result is anxiety: our fast-moving technological society has deprived people of unifying stories and myths, whether religious, ideological, or ecological.

Our growing knowledge undermines old belief systems and authorities while our ever-expanding freedom provides us with an almost unlimited set of lifestyle, career, hobby, and moral options. Without a clear foundation of values or ideologies to guide us, this array of choices is paralyzing. Without a firm sense of purpose, what career can we choose that will satisfy our desire for identity and meaning? Without a firm moral compass, how can we place lifestyle alternatives, such as drug use or respect for the environment, in the proper context?

Individual human beings, cut off from the social and natural "objects" that surround them, shorn of their faith but possessing a mantle of freedom, confront a multitude of complex, fragmented roles and choices. "This," Rollo May observes, "is why anxiety is so profoundly connected with the problem of freedom. If the individual did not have some freedom, no matter how minute, to fulfill some new potentiality, he would not experience anxiety. The existentialist philosopher Sören Kierkegaard described anxiety as 'the dizziness of freedom.'"[2] In the kind of world typified by trend two, where freedom of all kinds, political as well as economic, is on the rise, this dizziness seems certain to evolve into mass vertigo.

The solution to this problem is as straightforward as it is difficult: the exercise of will through self-empowerment. The knowledge era may ease such an agenda by enhancing the level of meaning and self-control available in the lives of individuals—in short, by *empowering* people.

A Habit of Alienation

On the road to transcendence and empowerment, however, a second major psychological challenge of the knowledge era crops up, a natural complement to anxiety: alienation.

Perhaps the dominant psychological reaction to the transition to a knowledge era is a growing sense of alienation in both the industrial and developing countries. Stripped of familiar moral, social, and political landmarks, caught up in the swift current of the knowledge era (or left stumbling in its wake), people in both the industrial and developing worlds are experiencing new kinds and intensities of personal and group alienation. For one thing, the death of ideologies has put an end to many of the unifying themes we use to combat estrangement. Many observers have commented on the decline of the sacred, of national and religious myths, even of the socialist ideal as ideas that stand against the void.

An equally powerful cause of alienation has to do with the challenge of coping with a knowledge-rich age: information overload. People can feel helpless in the midst of a bewildering array of information. A specific result is to imbue the knowledge era with an unprecedented degree of social complexity—a third route to alienation. Social issues, their characteristics as well as causes and cures, seem more complicated than ever before. This complexity is exacerbated by the frightening speed and degree of change in the knowledge era and by the pervasiveness of abstract realities. Abstraction may well be the governing principle of a knowledge era: knowledge, which represents ideas rather than things, is inherently abstract, and an era in which society and economy revolve around knowledge and information is bound to become ever more abstract—a process accelerated by fragmentation, relativism, and the crisis of authority.

A global media age also alienates people from what is perhaps the most important measure of psychological stability and personal grounding: a firm sense of place, physical as well as social. Joshua Meyrowitz discussed this phenomenon in his insightful book *No Sense of Place*. "At one time," he wrote, "physical presence was a prerequisite for first-hand experience. To see and hear a president speak in his office, for example, you had to be with him in his office." This, of course, is no longer the case. "The evolution of media has decreased the significance of physical presence in the experience of people and events."³ Our ability to locate ourselves in the world may be weakened by electronic media's constant assault on our sense of personal and social place.

The forces of alienation in our age are undoubtedly manifold, but the knowledge era is double-edged. It presents not merely the risk of an alienation at least as profound as that of the industrial era, but also a prospect for escape from alienation to an unprecedented degree. The knowledge era seems likely to impel the further spread of economic and political freedom throughout the world, providing individuals with stunning educational and entertainment options. In the final analysis, through its effect on the workplace and other social institutions, it can and should be about the empowerment of individual human beings. In the process, human alienation—from nature, from society, from self—would give way to new levels of connectedness and satisfaction.

The Pessimism Syndrome

A particular danger emerges in our age because of the naturally pessimistic bias of a prevalent and important media. It is well known that the media have a broad tendency to report negative or pessimistic stories for their shock value, which benefits ratings. At the same time, in the knowledge era the relative balance between knowledge that we acquire through personal knowledge or contact and the knowledge that we obtain through external accounts is thrown off balance. Our personal observations seem to count for little against the vast wave of information sweeping over us each day in a dozen forms, swamping our perceptions and washing away the familiar landmarks of our experience.

> **Together these phenomena produce the pessimism syndrome: the pervasive tendency to think things are getting precipitously worse when they are not.**

People have always sought to understand the world around them. In an information age that understanding comes primarily from news outlets, whether print, broadcast, or online. And people who listen exclusively to the press may well believe that the world is going under.

Surprise Scenario:
An Alienation-Based Demagogue

Among the dangers posed by the knowledge era, one of the most disturbing is the ability of a new kind of demagogue to take advantage of the disenchantment produced by globalization, rapid change, economic uncertainty, and alienation to promote hatred, scapegoating, and coercion. This risk is as real in Mexico as elsewhere.

In this scenario, a knowledge-era demagogue emerges in Mexico. A knowledge-era provocateur could break the mold of industrial-era demagogues. He or she could appeal to a regional or global rather than local or national audience, represent a high-tech rather than a backward constituency and ideology, make sophisticated use of twenty-first century propaganda techniques, and take advantage of the pluralism of views and relativism of modern societies to legitimate new ideas.

Much of the dissatisfaction that this demagogue could exploit is already producing pseudo-demagogues on national stages. What is missing is a trigger—a precipitating spark for the spread of disquieting views. The most likely trigger is the emergence of serious and persistent economic hardship. A severe recession in Mexico could expand the would-be demagogue's base of support, with a number of chilling outcomes. Any of the following results are possible:

- **Minority groups are discriminated against and persecuted as scapegoats** as they are blamed for the economic decline. A demagogue could try to direct the resentments of a frustrated middle-class against poor farmers in rural areas.

- **The country's democratic transition** is interrupted as a demagogic government quashes dissent.

- **Wide-ranging state economic planning, protectionism, and mercantilism return** as the demagogue seeks answers to economic problems. This strategy would appear readily, given the Mexican government's traditional role in the economy.

- **Tensions with the United States increase** as the demagogue finds objects for scapegoating beyond the country's borders. This risk is especially great if the United States faces a large-scale recession and the rise of its own demagogues.

"Television is now, indisputably, the primary source of news for most Americans," argues David Shaw in the *Los Angeles Times*. "It may also be the primary source of the cynicism that increasingly pervades the news media and society at large." Shaw continues with a neat summary of the present hypothesis:

> Just as studies have shown that viewers who see crime-dominated local TV news shows are likely to think that crime is much more prevalent than it really is, so viewers who watch national news shows, magazine shows and the weekend political talk shows are likely to think that the world in general, and politicians in particular, are much worse than they really are.[4]

Confronted with such an unrelenting tide of pessimism, it is no wonder that Americans, as well as the citizens of many other industrialized nations, are depressed about both the state of their societies and their future prospects, even as they see little evidence of catastrophe around them. The message delivered to most Americans is that things are bad and the future holds enormous peril. Robert Samuelson phrases it this way: "When surveyed, about four-fifths of us say we are satisfied with our own lives. But when asked about the country—whether it's 'moving in the right direction'—Americans are routinely glum." This perceptual gap "has been true for at least two decades. Somehow, a society that satisfies most of us most of the time has also convinced many of us that it's rolling inexorably toward the edge of a cliff."[5]

Partly, then, this phenomenon involves a divergence in confidence about the present and the future, a creeping suspicion that even if things look good for the moment, they will soon turn for the worse. But it also implies a fear that general social trends, and in particular the economic situation, are running in negative directions, even when evidence from people's own lives suggests otherwise. The prevalence of the pessimism syndrome calls into question our certainty in making the transition to a new era of human affairs and contributes to personal stress and depression. The syndrome could have broader social effects as well: it could stifle entrepreneurship and progress and undermine faith in the ability of social institutions to address problems. It could feed anxieties about the future that could undermine future proposals for free trade. And ultimately, it could drive

Figure 25
Americans' Perceptions of Broad Social Trends, 1988–1995

Percentage of Americans who say they are satisfied or dissatisfied with "the way things are going in the country"

Source: Frank Luntz, "The American Dream: Renewing the Promise," survey analysis for the Hudson Institute, December 8, 1995, mimeo.

Americans into the arms of politicians promising solutions to problems that do not really exist, or at least not to the degree people think.

Human Psychology in Mexico: A Resilient Culture

The psychological stresses that Mexico confronts today are obvious enough. Globalization and "convergence with the world" seem to threaten the human need for security. The pace of change in Mexico, which is tied to the U.S. economic and cultural juggernaut, is probably faster than in many other developing countries. The sort of issues presented by trend five, which cut the foundation out from under peoples' senses of identity and security, pose an intense challenge for Mexico over the next decade.

> At the same time, the knowledge era is a time of opportunity as well as challenge. Over the next decade Mexico can become a country enjoying notably greater prosperity and dignity and achievement. The key is to manage change well.

In the past Mexico lurched from savior to savior in its effort to address areas of conflict in the national psyche. The current movement toward an open, democratic, accountable system makes possible the creation of a more robust system, based on personal strength and the willingness of individuals to assume responsibility for the country's future. But the transition remains fraught with danger: forfeiting one's illusions about charismatic leaders along with everything else is a traumatic prospect. If the knowledge era is an age of the "empowered individual," the cultures and political systems that have traditionally shunned individualism will perhaps confront the most wrenching social and psychological transition.

Alienation: Sources and Evidence

In theory Mexicans confront the same daunting lineup of trauma and alienation as the citizens of any other nation in our transitional age. The shocks of modernization, liberalization, and other forms of change pulled by the engines of history are rocking the country as it races through the industrial era into the knowledge era. There is the simultaneous process of globalization and pluralism, which exaggerates the impact of modernization and undermines core elements of human identity, such as place and community. There is the fact that all of these changes are accelerating and becoming more far-reaching with each decade.

Perhaps most of all, there is the assault on authority structures and value systems. Political parties, governmental institutions, traditional cultures, the church, the family, schools—it is difficult to think of an authority structure in Mexico or elsewhere in the world that is not under enormous strain with the transition to a knowledge era. In the precarious social order that results, alienation can become commonplace. In some cases the impact of social instability is only too real: recent polls have found, for example, that more than a quarter of all Mexicans were a victim, or had a relative who was a victim, of a crime in the previous three months.

Cynicism bred by decades of corrupt authoritarian rule in Mexico magnifies the era's natural bent toward alienation. Many Mexicans disdain their government and other social authorities. "It's all because of government corruption," one young Mexican business consultant told an interviewer during the 1998 financial crises; "they trick us and lie to us."[6] Here we find yet another reason why the country's transition to democracy is so important: it can help to alleviate a major source of social alienation.

This creates a truly classic context for anxiety in Mexico. Traditional moral and institutional anchors are drifting; the boundaries of choice—in politics, business, religion, lifestyle, and a dozen other areas—are dissolving; the "dizziness of freedom" will not go away. In the years ahead Mexicans will have a number of decisions to make that will set the course of the nation for decades to come, but they will have few reassuring values or authorities to guide them. These are disturbing trends in a country where a habit of alienation was already well established: as Octavio Paz writes, the Mexican "builds a wall of indifference and remoteness between reality and himself, a wall that is no less impenetrable for being invisible. The Mexican is always remote, from the world and from other people. And also from himself."[7]

Several recent studies have clarified the ways in which these stressful trends are inducing anxiety's counterpart, broad-based social alienation. One recent survey at the National Autonomous University of Mexico (UNAM) found a significant level of psychological upheaval among Mexicans, especially those with less education. Recent changes in Mexico—from modernization to globalization to democratization to liberalization—have "occurred in a climate of tension," one report on the study's results concludes, creating a "contradiction between values, attitudes and opinions, especially as Mexican society approaches a free-market economy with formal democracy. These contradictions are even more apparent as they attempt to co-exist with traditional ways of life and thinking."[8]

Massive political change in a country where the bulk of the populace is uninterested in politics is bound to generate confusion, anxiety, and uncertainty. People are now asked to make decisions that previously were made for them. One result is that Mexicans frequently opt for practices and institutions that are familiar—for example, even after competition was introduced, 80 percent of telephone users stuck with the state-owned Telmex company for long-distance service. In this regard the UNAM study found a disturbing contradiction between expressed support for democracy and willingness to build a legitimate civic culture: "Mexicans of the [19]90s do not widely seek to participate in the political process," a report on the study noted, "and remain skeptical of society, and in particular, of the government."[9]

Another major study undertaken in part by staff from the Mexican Institute of Psychiatry similarly found growing "mental upheaval and anguish" throughout the society, especially among the young, the old, and the disenfranchised. This study tied what it called a recent growth in mental illness to economic strains (resulting from the 1995 peso crisis) and social violence. But broader anxieties connected with the transition to a new era, manifested in such forms as workplace tensions, played a role as well. The researchers found that one in four Mexicans is susceptible to some form of mental disturbance; fully 16 percent of those studied displayed significant levels of anxiety at the level of panic attacks and similar disorders; 13 percent suffered from severe depression. Only a very small proportion of those suffering from such illnesses had consulted specialists.[10]

Keeping Alienation in Check

Unlike in some other developing nations, however, there are good reasons to expect psychological stress and alienation in Mexico to remain in check. Of course, personal anxiety can be expected to rise here as it is everywhere during this anxious period. Measures of psychological disorders may also continue to increase, and this category of illness will come to be seen as a major health crisis. But this trend may be less likely to produce mass social instability or bitter reactions to globalization than elsewhere, at least among members of the middle class. Mexican culture benefits from a number of protections against alienation that will help it to cope fairly well with the psychological challenges of the next decade.

The most important protection is the family. A strong family structure ameliorates alienation to some degree and offers a life raft against rapid change. Mexicans frequently remark that Americans are alienated and disconnected in comparison to the sense of grounding and belonging that is offered by Mexican family life. Yet as participants in trend five, Mexicans do suffer from the same global weakening of families as is at work in the United States, and this could contribute to growing alienation.

Nor is Mexico a stranger to global-local interactions, an accelerated pace of change, and other traits of the transition to the knowledge era. Modern Mexican culture rests on a foundation of massive social change, and Mexicans (at least of the educated urban variety) frequently remark that they feel perfectly at home in a world of cross-cutting cultural influences. This furnishes the country with an important psychological advantage over cultures that are more insular in their mind-set. Postmodern, postmaterialist values are more advanced in Mexico than elsewhere in Latin America.

Even the famous cynicism of Mexicans can help control alienation by keeping expectations in check. The phenomenon of rising expectations so common in developing nations at times of transition may not emerge in Mexico during the next decade, because Mexicans are too jaded to let their expectations run wild. Hard experience with failed reforms and unfulfilled promises may help them keep their hopes to a minimum, so that their actual experience exceeds expectations.

In broad terms, then, the same level of psychological stress, anomie, and alienation may not develop in Mexico over the next decade as in such places as the Republic of Korea, China, or even the United States.

It is worth stressing, too, that for Mexico the knowledge era offers a powerful means of countering anxiety and alienation even as it threatens to exacerbate them. Empowered, self-directed, prosperous, knowledgeable people—true citizens of the knowledge era—do not suffer from the same degree of alienation. One reason for the walls of indifference and despair that Octavio Paz has so poignantly described has been the country's lack of freedom and a corresponding absence of trust. With Mexico's democratic opening and economic liberalization—processes inherent in its postmodern transition—the opportunity will come for individuals to break down these walls and engage with fellow citizens in the participatory, democratic building of a new society. If these trends continue, the knowledge era and its hallmarks could become Mexico's best answer to alienation.

In the process, however, Mexicans will undergo a period of intense psychological challenge. Any optimism about Mexico's ability to meet the challenges of this trend must be qualified in important ways, because Mexico will hardly be immune from the twin psychological burdens of a transitional period and the unfolding knowledge era itself. Surveys already indicate growing mental anguish, and this trend cannot be ignored.

The risks are particularly great for those segments of society left behind by the onrushing engine of socioeconomic progress. By far the most precarious aspect of Mexico's national psychology over the next decade stems from the risk that globalization and democratization will widen the already yawning socioeconomic chasm. Those in Mexico likely to be hardest hit by psychological stress are those who are most alienated from the economic, social, and political mainstream: the urban and (even more so) the rural poor. One can imagine a disturbing scenario in which better-off Mexicans are drawn into the advancing globalizing sector of the economy and participate actively in the country's burgeoning democracy, while the majority of the rural poor and many of their urban counterparts find themselves shut out of the "modern" Mexico. If this comes to pass, Mexico's poor will pay a high psychological price—and the country could well pay a major social price as well, in the form of accelerating unrest in the countryside, worsening crime in the cities, and a spreading drug trade.

These dangers highlight the importance of easing inequality in Mexico and reaching out to the poor with the educational and economic opportunities that will allow them to be part of the emerging knowledge era. Several recent studies have found levels of mental illness to be much higher among the poor and disenfranchised; childhood malnutrition, for example, seems connected to mental illness. Expanding the psychological treatment available to poor Mexicans will be a crucial means for addressing the knowledge era's risks of alienation.

The struggle to overcome alienation is intimately related to the process of economic and political institution-building that is part of other trends. Much of the famed cynicism and fatalism of Mexicans—their "ageless conviction that danger is just around the corner," as Carlos Fuentes puts it, "in a lost bullet, a casual encounter, a burst of anger, in sickness, in hunger, in bondage"[11]—stems from endlessly inefficient, dishonest, and brutal authoritarian governments. Creating social institutions inside and outside of government that can win public trust is a key step toward the country's psychological healing. This same process may, in a fairly short time, end up transforming characteristics commonly regarded as essential components of "Mexican culture": social institutions worthy of trust will create a trusting society; stronger rule of law will awaken the entrepreneurial spirit.

The Role of the Media

Like many other developing nations, Mexico is something of a case study in the influence of the pessimism syndrome. It is too early to tell, however, whether the syndrome is temporary or permanent and what kind of effect it will have on the country's development.

The Mexican media today definitely emphasize the scandalous aspect of stories. Combined with a minimal level of professionalism among journalists and widespread cynicism, this perspective creates an environment in which very little truly optimistic (or even accurate) news is reported. In what is perhaps a natural result of democracy, the Mexican press, released from the yoke of an authoritarian political system, is testing the limits of freedom. Reporting on the most scandalous and controversial stories has become a sort of badge of honor. In the process the role of the media has turned 180 degrees, from the optimistic, insipid, pro-government line of previous decades to the ultimate extreme in cynicism and bad taste. Although there is little direct survey evidence, anecdotal evidence from observers of the Mexican scene (including pollsters) supports the view that the average literate Mexican assumes that the situation is more ominous than it actually is. Although relatively few Mexicans read newspapers or magazines on a regular basis and many do not own televisions, all forms of media will continue to penetrate Mexican society during the next decade—potentially encouraging the full flowering of the pessimism syndrome.

Throughout the industrial and developing world, education is a critical support for those who are experiencing unprecedented historical transformations while being bombarded with the negative bias of the media. This is especially true in Mexico. In the UNAM study of values in the 1990s, 60 percent of those opposed to the privatization effort had no formal education; the majority of Mexicans with a university degree supported the process and fewer than 30 percent of them opposed it. "This same difference in responses was seen in all responses to economic issues," one report explained, "where people with high incomes and/or high education differed notably from those with low income and/or little education."[12]

These numbers provide stark evidence of the virtuous and vicious cycles at stake in psychological efforts to cope with change and of the urgency of Mexico's race against time.

Over the next decade, higher levels of educational achievement, a growing middle class, and continued robust economic growth could create a supportive virtuous cycle that will do much to keep the reform process on track. If, on the other hand, secondary and higher education graduation rates remain largely unchanged while the middle class absorbs relatively few new members, the potential will be great for social backlash to originate among undereducated groups who cannot comprehend the rationale for a painful reform process. The race is on to increase the amount of schooling the population receives and to furnish enough middle-class jobs to avoid a disastrous vicious cycle of social decay.

Notes

1. Nathaniel Branden, "Self-Esteem in the Information Age," in Frances Hesselbein et al., eds., *The Organization of the Future* (San Francisco: Jossey-Bass, 1997), 221.

2. Rollo May, *The Discovery of Being* (New York: W. W. Norton, 1983), 112.

3. Joshua Meyrowitz, *No Sense of Place: The Impact of Electronic Media on Social Behavior* (New York: Oxford University Press, 1985), vii, 125.

4. David Shaw, "Beyond Skepticism: Have the Media Crossed the Line Into Cynicism?" *Los Angeles Times,* April 19, 1996, p. A1.

5. Robert J. Samuelson, *The Good Life and Its Discontents: The American Dream in the Age of Entitlement* (New York: Times Books, 1995), 6.

6. Quoted in John Ward Anderson, "They Trick Us and Lie to Us," *Washington Post,* September 8, 1998, p. A17.

7. Octavio Paz, *The Labyrinth of Solitude and Other Writings,* trans. Lysander Kemp, Yara Milos, and Rachel Phillips Belash (New York: Grove Press, 1985), 29.

8. "Mexicans of the Nineties," *Este Pais*, September 1, 1996, trans. CSIS staff.

9. Ibid.

10. Ivonne Melgar, "Causes of our Mental Health Crisis," *Reforma*, April 25, 1998, trans. CSIS staff.

11. Carlos Fuentes, *A New Time for Mexico* (Berkeley: University of California Press, 1996), 20.

12. "Mexicans of the Nineties."

7 ■
Scenarios for Mexico's Development

THE FINAL ENDEAVOR OF THIS STUDY is to apply the trends driving world politics over the next decade to several representative scenarios for Mexico. The aim is not to forecast the future, but to furnish a sense of the range of outcomes that could develop as Mexico undergoes the transition to a knowledge era. These scenarios, rather than specifying one likely outcome, are intended to help government and business planners consider the implications of alternative visions of Mexico's future. As the promotional material from one of the world's leading scenario planning groups, at Royal Dutch Shell, suggests in a promotional pamphlet: "Scenarios are plausible and challenging stories, not forecasts. They do not extrapolate from the past to predict what will happen in the future, but instead offer . . . very different stories of how the future might look."

An important purpose of such stories is to provide a framework for understanding which scenario is in the process of emerging. Accordingly, each scenario includes a list of the most important indicators that point to its emergence. Individuals and organizations with a stake in Mexico's future are invited to use these snapshots of hypothetical futures to keep track of events, judge their character, and understand their likely course.

> These scenarios represent possible futures for Mexico's own internal society, politics, and economics; they remain to be tied to broader regional or global scenarios.

Some international connections are fairly obvious and have been highlighted in the preceding pages. Given Mexico's export dependence on the United States, for example, a prolonged recession north of the border could make strong economic growth in Mexico nearly impossible. Other regional or global influences with importance for Mexico's future include a reaction against reform and a return to old-style military or statist rule throughout Latin America. Exceedingly unlikely as this is, such a development could reverberate throughout Mexico, as would any sort of global economic catastrophe. Here, however, the focus is on developments within the country.

Importantly, the time frame at issue in the scenarios spans the next 7 to 10 years. All indicators listed for each scenario represent developments that could occur within the next decade. Other scenarios, such as "Industrial-World Mexico," are conceivable but not within the specified period. Some will question whether two of the more extreme scenarios treated here—"Democratic Mexico" and "Ungovernability"—could actually emerge within this time span. Although they are not the most likely outcomes, these two possibilities certainly deserve consideration; even if they have not emerged full-fledged by 2005 or even 2010, Mexico could be so far along the path to one or the other by then that one of them accurately describes the evolving reality.

On balance, there are reasons to be guardedly—with strong emphasis on "guardedly"—optimistic about Mexico's prospects over the next decade. A number of major trends, such as the expansion of democracy and the emergence of environmentally friendly technologies, provide grounds for such optimism--but the strongest reason is the fact that, empowered by the technologies and information of the new era, the Mexican people have the ability to influence which scenario occurs. In the knowledge era more than ever before, people are not the prisoners of trends but their authors.

Still, it is crucial not to underestimate the scope of the challenge Mexico faces, or the intensity of its social transformation, or the embryonic nature of the institutions it so badly needs to see it through. The persistent reality of two Mexicos—one relatively prosperous, educated, and urbane; the other poor, rural, and often disconnected from the positive trends under way—calls into question the empowering character of the knowledge era. Today, only the fairly small middle class could be said to have the power to shape the trends of the new era to their benefit. Improved social equality may be a precondition for achieving the promise of the knowledge era. Likewise, the persistence of crime and corruption keeps alive a very real danger of widespread social instability.

Of the five scenarios proposed, three ("Muddling Through," "Losing Ground" and "Old Wine in New Bottles") are moderate extrapolations from the status quo in either a promising or discouraging direction. The remaining two ("Democratic Mexico" and "Ungovernability") represent positive and negative extremes of the same basic dichotomy. It is important to note that the scenarios are not completely independent; they could emerge serially, one after another. In a sense, the major risk in Mexico over the next decade is that "Losing Ground" will mutate into "Old Wine in New Bottles," which would then generate "Ungovernability"; short-term indicators for the first two scenarios, then, might be clues to the long-term emergence of the third, even though society-wide chaos remains unlikely.[1]

Scenario One: Democratic Mexico

This scenario involves the acceleration of the democratic transition, the continuation of robust economic growth, the creation of a notably larger middle class, and the positive effect of these developments on other trends. It is significant for its difference in kind rather than degree from the status quo:[2] It assumes that democratization and liberalization accelerate, economic growth improves even from the very encouraging 1996–1997 levels, a vibrant small and medium-sized business sector emerges, and Mexicans continue to thrive at the intersection of global-local trends, where the citizens of so many other countries feel bewildered and alienated. The indispensability of a good economic performance to this scenario means that (in contrast to the next three scenarios) it can be understood, in a sense, as a "fast-growth scenario."

> Another way of putting it is that the "Democratic Mexico" scenario represents the achievement of virtuous cycles and the avoidance of vicious ones.

Millions of new job seekers over the next decade will have to find meaningful employment, expanding the tax-paying, savings-enhancing middle class. Mexican institutions will gain increasing control over society, allowing for more economic progress, more faith in government, and in turn ever more effective institutions. Greater access to information will allow people to counteract, rather than succumb to, the sensationalistic impulses of the media. Mexico's service sector will be strengthened, in both the domestic and the export arenas. In the broadest sense, then, this scenario represents a world in which Mexico's democratic transition works to alleviate social ills—in the way advocates of democracy hope—rather than to exacerbate them through demagoguery and corruption, as some pessimists fear.

This scenario does not assume that everything turns out well. Unemployment and inequity would remain major social challenges; tensions associated with globalization would persist; corruption and drug trafficking would continue. No magic wand will wave away Mexico's challenges, and this scenario does not assume the existence of one. It merely assumes that nearly all major social and economic indicators begin to move in the right direction and at a pace notably better than the status quo. "Democratic Mexico" remains very much a work in progress.

Along with strong economic growth, an essential precondition for this scenario is muscular and increasingly (though in our time frame, not completely) corruption-free, credible institutions—from the Congress to the police, the courts, and the military. These institutions should be able to get a better handle on the three daggers pointing at the heart of Mexican progress: crime, corruption, and narcotrafficking. Closing the gap between social and economic development and political institutions remains as important a task today as it was when Samuel Huntington famously outlined the importance of this gap in the late 1960s.[3] Besides these three herculean tasks assigned to Mexico's nascent institutions of democratic governance, there are other, equally crucial ones, most notably an improved legal foundation for the economy, as outlined in chapter 3.

Sergio Sarmiento has described some aspects of such a scenario. "Mexico is becoming freer, both economically and politically," and a national transformation "now looks inevitable. Provided Mexico's changes take place with a minimum of violence and opposition, the country should be well-placed to join the community of democratic, developed nations in the next century."[4] Even the thoroughly pessimistic Jorge Castañeda has written that, if "all goes well," Mexico's "social configuration will begin to look like the United States' sometime in the middle of the next century."[5]

Politically, then, this scenario assumes Mexico's arrival as an increasingly stable and mature democracy, with declining threats of reaction or rollback from the gains of political or economic liberalization. It assumes maturing forms of political participation, from voting to protesting to distributing leaflets. And it describes a world in which, as many observers of the Mexican scene have hoped, democratic accountability helps to solve many of the country's problems, with the government acting on such issues as inequity, environmental protection, the rule of law, and corruption.

Regionally, this scenario witnesses improved relations between Mexico and its neighbors. A strong economic performance and the emergence of a larger middle class will reduce the pressure for illegal immigration to the United States, swell the market for U.S. exports, and otherwise establish Mexico as a stable, reliable partner. Meanwhile, Mexican achievements in growth and liberalization could enhance its image to the south, perhaps fostering talks on association with the Mercosur group. Long-simmering notions of some sort of free trade pact with the European Union might take on more meaning. At the same time, regional cooperation on cross-border issues, from the environment to drug smuggling, will increase substantially.

A variant of this scenario is the emergence of the decentralized, human-scale political model of communities as favored by Carlos Fuentes.

In this subscenario, political and economic freedom could combine with Mexico's traditions of local governance and community to allow towns, villages, and cities to assume a large share of the power now wielded by higher levels of government. A thorough social pluralism could result as different regions experiment with different forms of social organization. Within our time frame this political evolution seems unlikely, given the still dominant role of Mexico City in national life. Wide disparities in wealth and social progress mean that any program of decentralization will have to allow for a substantial redistributive role on the part of the federal government; some observers worry that localism could easily slide into tense regionalism. Nonetheless, a program of growing local influence corresponds well to the demands of the knowledge era.

Indicators of Scenario One: Democratic Mexico

- Elections at all levels are judged to be more open and more competitive, and major parties accept the results. Measures of society-wide political participation—demonstrations, campaigning, referenda, and the like—increase. The PRI shift to open primaries continues.

- Congress acquires growing powers and larger staffs and exercises an oversight role over the executive.

- The principle of reelection is introduced into the legislature and, eventually, all levels of government.

- Regionalism is partly resolved by strong efforts on the part of PAN and PRD to become truly national parties. PAN candidates, for example, win in more southern cities.

- Growing political decentralization is productive, transferring more functions to lower levels of government.

- More governorships change hands from one party to another. Governors of all parties turn increasingly to professional technocrats to staff their administrations.

- Reports of corruption at top levels of government give way to second-order corruption scandals at lower levels, giving the impression that corruption is partly under control and will ebb over time.

- Measures of information penetration—telephones, wireless communications, the Internet, television—burgeon.

- Public opinion polls show slight but notable growth in public confidence in governmental institutions and optimism about the future. Measures of intersocial trust rise. Media sensationalism declines.

- Economic growth runs consistently at 6 to 7 percent or greater; no major financial crises occur. Mexico's commitment to free trade expands and include discussions with Mercosur and the EU.

- Evidence mounts of the health of civil society, especially regarding the effectiveness and number of nongovernmental organizations, the role of religion, and the level of personal voluntarism.

- Economic growth generates enough jobs for new workers. Official unemployment remains below 5 percent. Employment by the informal sector of the economy declines to 20 percent or less.

- The middle class grows to 30 percent or more of the population.

- New nonhierarchical, decentralized, innovative business management practices begin to influence society.

- Socioeconomic inequity declines, if ever so slightly, as indicated by such measurements as income and wealth distribution and wages.

- Mexican firms gain an increasing share of exports leaving the country relative to that of foreign-owned multinationals. The amount and sophistication of Mexican exports grow.

- The Mexican central bank achieves greater influence and independence.

- Economic and financial transparency increases, beginning with the banking sector.

- The proportion of GDP generated by small and medium-sized firms grows steadily. The government assists these firms' growth.

- Oil production grows with the help of new outside investment and privatization.

- The educational system shows signs of improvement at all levels, partly through increased funding.

- Savings rates match and exceed government targets, moving toward 25 percent or more of GDP.

- Privatization accelerates; petrochemical sell-offs go forward successfully.

- The state-dominated proportion of GDP gradually declines.

- Police professionalism is enhanced. The levels of crime, especially violent crime, plateau and begin to decline.

- Illegal immigration to the United States declines.

- Regional cooperation on immigration, environmental, and drug issues grows.

- Major progress is made on environmental issues. Investments in remediation grow substantially and levels of air and water treatment rise. Mexico City takes steps to get its water crisis under control.

Scenario Two: Muddling Through

"Muddling Through" is the scenario closest to the status quo. It is a world in which things do not get notably worse, but neither do any breakthroughs occur in such areas as economic reform or democratization. Things continue more or less as they have been for the last three or four years.

In brief, what that means is that "Muddling Through" is a mildly optimistic scenario.

"Muddling Through" assumes that major social collapse, an attack on reform by old-guard PRI dinosaurs, or other possibly disastrous events do not come to pass. It assumes that the modest economic progress of the last four years, recovering from the 1994 peso collapse, continues: more jobs are created, the financial sector grows healthier, foreign investment continues, privatization proceeds. Politically, it assumes that Mexico's nascent democracy remains in place and that it functions at least well enough to prevent social gridlock.

And yet this scenario, like Mexico's current condition, offers many reasons for worry, because it also assumes that the country does not take major steps toward solving its numerous challenges. Incremental progress continues in a number of areas, such as environmental protection and weeding out corruption, but it remains an open question how long incrementalism will be able to hold off social unrest.

Put another way, this scenario assumes that major social institutions will neither become much more effective nor degrade noticeably. Seven or eight years from now the degree of rule of law, social crime, penetration by drug-related corruption of the government and military, and other measures of stable governance remain much as they are today. The implication, of course, is that underlying forces—the actual power of narcotraffickers, levels of public disaffection, corporate frustration with lax economic regulations and enforceable contracts—have been moving in a profoundly disturbing direction and will ultimately cause mischief, even though the outward signs of institutionalization have not seemed to change. This is an important example of how dependent Mexico is on positive progress: even the mildly negative scenario of stagnation has the potential (some would say guarantee) of declining into social instability.

Meanwhile, relations with the United States bounce along on the same roller coaster of friendly rhetoric and sudden controversy that they have been on since 1994. From drug smuggling to immigration to financial reform, the scenario assumes that the major issues in the relationship do not show signs of marked deterioration—but they do not improve noticeably either. Meanwhile, Mexico's relations with its neighbors to the south and with other potential trading partners (such as the European Union) show little change.

By and large, then, this scenario embodies a projection of the status quo; its fundamental indicator is therefore that events move forward with relatively little major change.

Indicators of Scenario Two: Muddling Through

- Most aspects of economic reform and privatization continue at more or less the same rate as today.

- Economic growth runs at 4.5 to 5 percent.

- Greater institutionalization and accountability in the economic field, such as autonomy of the central bank and transparency of financial transactions, continue to show halting progress.

- Bank failures occur from time to time, but in broad terms the effort to enhance bank capitalization and address problem loans moves forward.

- Politically, the turbulence of recent years continues with no major breakthrough: no opposition candidate wins the presidency, nor does the PRI return to old-style national dominance.

- Elections remain fairly free and honest as they have been in recent rounds.

- Disputes and brinkmanship continue between the PRI presidency and the opposition Congress, but—as in recent months—both sides recognize the danger of gridlock, and legislation makes its way through on a number of key areas.

- Violence in Chiapas continues; it does not explode on the national scene, but nor does a major settlement emerge.

- Environmental protection improves very gradually, with the lack of major investments remaining a substantial barrier to more dramatic advances.

- Narcotrafficking continues at current or perhaps slightly increased levels.

Scenario Three: Losing Ground

"Losing Ground" represents the victory of stagnation and the beginning of a slow reversal of the economic, legal, and environmental progress of recent years. This scenario assumes that the fundamental conflicts in Mexican society—between mercantilism and liberalism, authoritarianism and democracy, equality and oligarchy—are not resolved to the extent that they are in the previous scenarios. Instead, action gets bogged down in political and economic disputes, producing a stalemated society. This pattern is accompanied by incomplete or little economic reform, which leaves the domestic industrial sector in a precarious position. A host of economic indicators, from unemployment to savings rates to the role of small and medium-sized firms, show little or no gain. Mediocre economic performance (and stagnant oil production) in turn leaves the government with insufficient revenues for the dozens of social investments that are crucial to the nation's future, especially in the areas of health and education. It is a notably more pessimistic scenario than "Muddling Through," which presumes at least a limited degree of progress.

As the basis for political gridlock and degeneration, this scenario foresees a nearly perpetual standoff between the remains of the PRI (or a resurgent PRI, which is suggested by a handful of signs today) and the emerging PAN and PRD, neither of which can ever gain true national stature or the president's office. The scenario assumes either that the PRI remains discredited and unable to recapture a dominant role in national political life, or that, if a revitalized PRI comes roaring back to national leadership, it does so with an agenda that would not so much turn the clock back on economic and political reform as keep it from moving forward.

This scenario would be especially likely, then, if Mexico's democratic process proves harmful rather than helpful to solving major social problems. If persistent legislative-executive standoffs produce policy gridlock, if angry and partisan debate destroys the potential for meaningful action on social equity and environmental protection, if big-money interests subvert the popular will on these and other issues, then contrary to the hopes of reformers Mexico's halfway democracy might turn out to delay rather than accelerate the development of a truly "democratic Mexico." This scenario could be realized if there are no counterproductive byproducts of democratization. Democracy could continue to evolve, contributing at the margins to solving a problem or two, but overall social, economic, and political trends would remain stuck in the mire of recent years.

Gerardo Otero has spelled out a possible variant of this scenario, which he calls "social liberalism."[6] This involves a less-than-democratic alliance of PRI-PAN technocrats, which pushes neoliberal economic policies ahead but is not as enthusiastic about political reform. By its nature this alliance addresses issues of concern to northern Mexico, but does little to head off rising instability and discontent in the south and southeast. This is one example of how "Losing Ground" could generate increased north-south regional tensions as an important byproduct. Although Otero does not say it, such an alliance could also pursue a halfway approach to privatization and other crucial elements of the liberalization plan, thus failing to achieve the full advantages of reform.

In fact, the danger of "Losing Ground" is that it might not (indeed, could not) last forever. It may well constitute a halfway point to something worse—such as "Old Wine in New Bottles" or "Ungovernability."

Because of the expectations attached to emerging democracy and a liberal economic system, and also because of major social strains just below the surface of such issues as inequity and corruption, stumbling along without major progress and beginning a long, slow cycle of decline is almost certain to lead to instability. There could come a point at which the weight of unfulfilled expectations is too great for the system to bear, a point at which this scenario would generate something else: widespread reaction and renewal of old politics, for example, or encroaching social chaos.

Beyond Mexico's borders this scenario would likely play out in a gradual heightening of tensions with the United States, as a host of important bilateral issues (immigration, drug smuggling, U.S. appeals for a stronger rule of law and business protections in Mexico) went unattended. Meanwhile, Mexico's plans for broader economic ties with Latin America, Europe, and Asia, as well as its larger hopes for regional cooperation on cross-border issues, would make little progress.

Indicators of Scenario Three: Losing Ground

- Mexico makes little or no progress on major economic reform tasks, especially financial sector accountability and transparency.

- The central bank's recent trend toward greater independence and influence is interrupted.

- Economic growth takes place at unspectacular levels, in the range of 3 to 4 percent.

- This level of growth provides a substantial number of new jobs, perhaps half a million annually, but not nearly enough to match the need generated by demographic trends. As a result, unemployment grows to 10 percent or more, and the informal sector's share of overall employment actually increases.

- Some major elections continue to generate widespread protests of irregularities. Political participation in voting and nonvoting forms perhaps begins to decline.

- Survey results demonstrate growing disaffection with the political and economic system, increasing alienation, and stagnant or declining levels of intersocial trust. Media sensationalism continues to undermine hope for the future and perceptions of progress.

- Congress does not approve presidential budgets in a timely fashion; repeated budgetary stalemates wrack the legislature. Constant standoffs with the executive branch often paralyze government decisionmaking.

- Governors rely on professional politicians rather than on experts and technocrats to run their administrations.

- Corruption scandals continue at all levels of government. Public confidence in government remains low.

- The PRI's move in the direction of open primaries and more accountability, and the trend toward modernists in the PRI, slows considerably.

- Information penetration increases only slightly.

- Bank failures continue and accelerate. Domestic capital is unavailable for business, crippling SMEs.

- Planned investments in environmental protection are delayed or canceled. Measures of air and water quality do not improve notably. A water crisis continues to threaten Mexico City, with no decisive action taken.

- The SME sector shows no noticeable improvement, and its share of GDP and exports does not increase.

- Little growth occurs in the middle class. Inequity persists and even grows as the new wealth coming into the country is not shared.

- Mexican firms do not gain a greater share of exports relative to foreign-owned multinationals. Overall exports do not increase, continue to lag behind in their level of technology and sophistication, and perhaps even begin to decline.

- Oil production stagnates; amid low world oil prices, government revenues and export earnings decline.

- Congress remains an adjunct player to the executive's dominant role in government.

- Few if any PAN candidates in the south or PRD candidates in north are elected.

- Privatization continues to generate much talk but little action. Petrochemical issues remain unresolved. Foreign capital infusions slow down. There is little increase in the technological level of Mexican industry.

- No improvements are evident in the educational system, especially in terms of the populations reached or their achievement.

- The state's role as a percentage of GDP holds more or less steady.

- Immigration and drug smuggling remain major irritants in Mexican-U.S. relations.

- No substantial cooperative regional ventures take place on cross-border environmental, drug, or other issues.

- Levels of crime remain high, neither worsening nor improving significantly.

Scenario Four: Old Wine in New Bottles

This scenario involves the return of the old guard—not necessarily the PRI, although its traditional tactics and goals would be employed. It represents a turning back of the clock on economic and political reform, a resurgence of some form of authoritarian rule, and a halt in privatization—in sum, a kind of recreation of the Mexican political and economic situation circa 1975 or 1980. Political reform is stifled and economic liberalization reversed, all with an eye toward recreating a "perfect dictatorship." Former U.S. ambassador to Mexico James Jones has noted the potential for such a scenario, worrying that "we're living on borrowed time. This generation of [Mexican] adults will probably survive on hope but I think over the next five to 10 years if that isn't translated into benefits and real opportunities, you're going to have demagogues rise up who want to turn the clock back."[7]

Politically, democratic contests for offices from the presidency to governorships and many local positions give way to the old style of Mexican politics: rigged campaigns, stuffed ballot boxes, bribed voters, and a presidency with final oversight on any election result in the country. The ruling party might absorb token losses in a few places to nurture the myth of a competitive democracy, but opposition parties are generally shut out of crucial election victories. Essential to this process is the revival of violent intimidation of regime opponents, whether they are journalists, members of human rights groups or other nongovernmental organizations, or opposition politicians.

Many observers of the Mexican scene argue that such an outcome is simply impossible—reform has proceeded too far, and the Mexican people have become too empowered, to permit such a thorough reversal of current trends.

This may be true, but such a scenario should not be ruled out. If it does occur, the now extended process of political opening and economic reform will probably ensure that it does not occur peacefully; many elements of Mexican society will react violently to being stripped of their new rights. Here is yet another avenue for the mutation of one scenario into another: a brief period of "Old Wine" could be followed by widespread social upheaval, or "Ungovernability." (A more hopeful—some would say quixotic—outcome would be the final and fundamental fragmenting of all elements holding together the status quo, opening the way ultimately for "Democratic Mexico.")

On the other hand, as is usually the case (though perhaps less so than several decades ago), a monolithic party attempting to reinstitute old methods of rule would find a number of allies in Mexican society, particularly if it cloaks its grab for power with the language of revolution, equality, and nationalism. In terms of the trend toward global tribes, this scenario is likely to come about as a nationalistic and perhaps class-based reaction to the pressures of globalization. It will therefore outline an agenda of real or mythical income redistribution, resistance to U.S. dictates, improved government-led health and educational systems, and perhaps even stronger environmental protection. And it will probably implement its reversal of democracy and economic liberalization in stages, so that it achieves solid control of the country before moving on to the final, most controversial gains.

Gerardo Otero has spelled out three variations of this scenario, which he calls "social reformism," "social economy," and "social democracy."[8] The first involves a resurgence of the state's role in the economy, led by socially conscious, but not especially democratic, PRIistas. The second modifies that outcome, perhaps in the form of a PRI-PRD alliance, which is not now in the cards; as a result, there are even greater statist interventions in areas such as land reform. Both versions favor and protect national businesses through new trade protectionism, though how this could be done within the confines of NAFTA is unclear. The third scenario envisions an outright PRD takeover of major national posts, including the presidency (although, given the tough experience of Cárdenas in the mayorship of Mexico City, this particular development seems unlikely as of mid-1998).

Efforts to improve income equity and environmental safeguards expand along with protectionism and industrial policy.

A possible variation of this scenario involves an unprecedented role for the military in a recentralized government structure.

Without a true transition to democracy, ills such as drug trafficking, crime, and corruption "could wear away the national patience, worsen the environment of daily life and even—as remote as it now seems—lead the military for the first time in half a century to claim a justification and right to power."[9] During the Zedillo years, troop strength has increased 15 percent and military spending by 16 percent—in the midst of government austerity measures.[10] Most observers view an outright military takeover as unlikely, but a partnership between the increasingly powerful military and old-style politicians is not out of the question in coming years, and it could give this scenario a repressive tinge.

Regionally, tensions with the United States will rise substantially in this scenario. The revisionist movement in Mexico is likely to welcome such tensions as a spur to its rule, and its probable actions—economic protectionism and antidemocratic repression—will certainly provoke sharp rebukes from the United States (and many Latin American states as well). The deteriorating cycle of hostility could even put NAFTA at risk.

Indicators of Scenario Four: Old Wine in New Bottles

- Old-guard candidates within PRD and PRI dominate those parties.

- Old political tactics return: election protests are common, and outside news reports talk about workers being bused to rallies. Old-guard candidates once again win with massive victories in the 80 to 90 percent range.

- New political alliances emerge between dinosaurs of PRI, PRD, and other political groupings.

- Democratic processes are interrupted. Signals of this include complaints from the press, warnings from outside human rights groups, and statements from the Catholic Church.

- All measures of political participation decline (except perhaps demonstrations against the reversals of democracy). Harassment of regime opponents expands.

- Mexican business discards new management models and reverts to old patterns of hierarchical control.

- Privatization is halted and reversed. The role of the state as percentage of GDP rises.

- The commitment to free trade wanes in favor of protectionism and industrial policy. NAFTA is imperiled, though the Mexican government would probably try to avoid this outcome.

- Exports stagnate and then begin to decline as one or more major outside investors end operations. The character of exports backtracks; there is greater dependence on oil and low-tech manufacturing.

- A banking crisis is reported to be serious, but lack of transparency prevents real accounting. The evidence of capital shortage is clear, however, including a lack of investment money for SMEs, which remain a small proportion of the overall economy.

- PAN is unable to extend its influence to central or southern portions of country.

- Crime continues at high levels and even worsens, generating new calls for social order.

- Illegal immigration to the United States increases. Many activists claim political asylum.

- Economic decisionmakers outside the presidency, including the central bank and the finance ministry, see their influence wane.

- Oil production begins a long, slow decline as Pemex is unable to obtain outside investments or new technology.

- The government declares its intention to make major social investment in areas such as health and education, and there is growing evidence that the government is giving massive subsidies to unemployed workers. But falling revenue means investments will actually decline and social tensions rise as a result.

- Corruption scandals are widespread, but as time goes on they are not always reported or protested inside Mexico. Foreign media dominate coverage. Reports of military corruption and ties to narcotraffickers rise both inside of and outside of the country.

- Official figures for unemployment, the informal sector, and other economic measures look favorable: 6 percent or less unemployment, for example. But unofficial figures are much higher, above 10 percent.

- Foreign direct investment plummets to a fraction of its current levels. Tensions grow between the multinationals already in place and the Mexican government.

- Financial and banking reform is shelved.

- Nationalist, anti-American rhetoric grows. Regional cooperation essentially comes to a halt.

- Evidence emerges of a closer alliance between the old guard and the military. It includes the influence of high-level military officers and the placement of top generals in key civilian posts.

Scenario Five: Ungovernability

This scenario contemplates the worst of all possible outcomes: the degeneration of Mexican society into violent chaos of the sort predicted by a handful of gloomy observers. The chaos can take a number of forms, which are spelled out in various subscenarios below. Although the indicators of this scenario vary depending on the subscenario that is emerging, some indicators are common to nearly all.

Although the sum of challenges and dangers in the coming decade seems to point to imminent social collapse, there are powerful factors related to Mexico's culture, history, and psychology that in fact make this scenario an extreme one.

Journalist Patrick Oster relates a story from the early 1980s in which a U.S. intelligence analyst charged with producing a new forecast of Mexico's future visited the country, reviewed its catalogue of social ills, and concluded that "Mexico was ripe to fall." His boss, the former CIA station chief in Mexico City, disagreed and rewrote the report: the younger analyst's mistake "had been to assume that Mexicans would react the same way that Americans would to such conditions," Oster explains. In fact, he continues, "Mexicans may complain vehemently and often about the ineptness and corruptness of their leaders," but that does not mean that social collapse or revolution is at hand. "The glass may be half-empty in Mexico, but it is also half-full." Among the Mexican people "there is patience and, most of all, an ability to endure."[11]

Like the "Democratic Mexico" scenario, this scenario represents a difference of kind rather than degree from the current situation. It demands an immense trigger—an economic depression, a massive new wave of social violence—to become reality. Although such an outcome cannot be completely ruled out, it is unlikely that crime, corruption, and unemployment at levels similar to those in the recent past could simply mutate into a fundamental revolution against the system. On the other hand, it is possible that the farther reform proceeds, the greater the expectations, engendering a danger that a sudden shock to the system will lead to social upheaval. And many of the subscenarios that follow might have their roots in the insurgencies now under way throughout the country, which could, over time, eat away more dramatically at the country's social fabric than they have done so far.

Neo-Medievalism

Perhaps the prototypical example of the neo-medieval subscenario is a Mexico in which central authority, and indeed all forms of authority, is rapidly waning and social chaos is gaining ground.

Michael Radu, one observer who considers the risk of a social collapse truly substantial, argues that "Mexico today is in deep, if not terminal, trouble." Even though past forecasts of collapse have been proved wrong, Mexico is "perilously on the verge of chaos and violence," he contends, and "the current crisis may well be the most dangerous. The reason is that virtually all of Mexico's historical cleavages—social, geographic, political, ethnic—seem to be converging at a moment when the central government is weaker than at any time since the revolution."[12] Comparing Mexico of the late 1990s to Colombia of the early 1980s, Radu concludes with a sober injunction: Mexico today "is not moving toward democracy or prosperity but toward instability and internal conflict."[13]

As its name implies, this subscenario involves the fragmentation of political authority into local or regional pieces, or into a complicated patchwork of rule involving government, business, the military, drug barons, and other actors. A corporate-narcotrafficker alliance might dominate in the north, while a highly dissolute residue of the central government holds sway over Mexico City and a combination of insurgent groups, military forces, and drug traffickers dominate in the south. Democracy is under assault everywhere, and coordinated action on issues such as inequity and environmental degradation comes to a halt. Mexico's economic fortunes and practices are as varied as its political rule, differing from region to region: some areas enjoy a kind of cowboy-capitalism prosperity, while others grow increasingly isolated and poor. There is no centrally directed process of reform and liberalization as there is today.

An interesting historical parallel might be early nineteenth-century Mexico, after the Revolution of 1810 gave way to a period of political banditry and violence during which Creole rulers could not consolidate a true nation. They "presided over a time of anarchy, economic impoverishment, the loss of national territory, and, above all, violence: revolutions, foreign interventions, civil struggles,"[14] as one historian has observed. Such broad-based social chaos will probably not emerge immediately from the current situation, but only after one or more scenarios of degradation have intervened. It will in any case have disastrous implications for Mexico's relations with its neighbors: for example, the emergence of this subscenario could generate a vicious cycle of growing U.S. border enforcement in response to the higher levels of illegal immigration and drug running, as well as declining U.S. investment. All of this would accelerate Mexico's rush into the abyss.

A possible variation of the collapse of social order is the fragmentation of the country along north-south lines.

Some segments of the population in the north and the capital resent their transfer payments to the poorer states of the country, and a few observers worry that these tensions could become destabilizing over time. Carlos Fuentes has called such a split between northern Mexico, "relatively prosperous, ever more modern, impulsive, decentralized, self-sufficient, well-informed, and integrated with the United States," and the southern states, "ever poorer, enslaved, without horizons," the "biggest danger I see in my country's future."[15] Such a split will not necessarily lead to violent disorder, the central hallmark of this subscenario; it could merely produce two (or more) autonomous areas. But the country's poor states, fearful of being abandoned and angry at the rejection of national unity, could lash out violently in reaction.

Vicious Capitalism

A variant of the neo-medieval outcome is one in which rapacious and unaccountable corporations emerge as a key social actor. Robert Kaplan has described Mexico as "*the* example of failing capacity in a state that is supremely subtle and middle-of-the-road." Kaplan quotes Mexican futurist Antonio Alonso as outlining a scenario involving the "destruction of current Mexican political institutions over the next decade, and the rise of local bosses and free-enterprise networks to replace them." Kaplan refers to such forms of corporate rule as "emerging neo-medieval principalities," claiming they are in the process of forming in areas such as Sinaloa, where government control is weak and business and drug groups are strong.[16]

This subscenario assumes that large corporations, both domestically and internationally owned, will become increasingly assertive once a broad process of social disintegration begins. Companies respond by taking control of certain parts of the country, beginning in the north, and imposing their own vision of social order. In such circumstances, concerns for social equity, labor rights, and environmental protection decline along with democratic accountability for business. But Mexico will remain interested in rapid economic growth and will attempt to pursue those aspects of national policy, including free trade, research and development, and foreign investment, that contribute to such a goal. This tense combination probably could not be sustained for long, however, and certainly not without the application of some degree of repressive force.

In fact, trends in Mexico are running in the direction of more, not less, social responsibility on the part of business. This subscenario does not assume that corporate leaders are somehow inherently evil, only that the collapse of order would magnify the desperate selfishness and will-to-power of all social actors, including corporations. Their role could then become threatening to democracy, liberalization, and long-term social order.

Social Revolution

This variant of "Ungovernability" represents a situation in which poverty and inequity worsen substantially, leading to a fairly traditional rebellion of a poor and disenfranchised majority against the power centers of the country. As in 1810, the revolution could be stoked by leftist church leaders, who condemn the evil of an inequitable society and furnish rebels with spiritual legitimacy. What occurs is not social fragmentation, as in "Neo-Medievalism," but a classic revolution that installs a coherent new central government into place.

> "Revolutions in Mexico are a desperate craving for order and protection," Carlos Fuentes has observed.[17] So they might be in the coming century: a search for security amid the knowledge era's tidal waves of change.

What such a revolution would mean in political and economic terms will depend, of course, on the character of the movement attaining power. Assuming that the movement involves a reaction against current trends, one can expect its agenda to be an extreme version of "Old Wine in New Bottles": statist control of the economy and society, (probably) a tight rein on political freedom, protectionism and nationalism, and so forth. Once such a rebellion is under way, however, just about any outcome could emerge from its confusing interplay of social forces. In fact, one could even imagine a moderate laissez-faire social revolution taking place against the undemocratic regime that wants to put "old wine in new bottles": a revolution that emphasizes liberal economics and democratic politics. Here, then, is an admittedly far-fetched mechanism by which one or more of the negative scenarios ends up producing "Democratic Mexico."

It is worth stressing again that this subscenario is unlikely. As long ago as the 1960s, and even in the wake of the student demonstrations of 1968, Octavio Paz chastened those who forecast another massive social revolution, claiming the possibility was remote. "The necessary social class, the historical protagonist, is lacking," he argued. Despite the country's stark socioeconomic divisions, "the regime has two weapons of dissuasion" to prevent a revolt—the army and social mobility:

> The former is odious but real; the latter is a decisive factor, a true safety valve. Because of this social mobility and other circumstances no less positive—distribution of lands, irrigation projects, et cetera—it would be absurd to say that the situation in the countryside is revolutionary.[18]

If anything, the country's relatively recent program of economic and political liberalization has opened this safety valve wider, furnishing Mexicans with the hope of a better future through reform, exports, education, national savings, and all the other benefits of development.

Yet although this outcome strikes most observers as virtually impossible in the twenty-first century, the country in fact may retain more elements of its revolutionary past than many like to think. Enrique Krauze describes a Mexico that "had turned its back on the past and primarily looked toward the future—but always with enormous cost and trouble and in modes that were ambiguous, uneven, and often contradictory," which he describes as leaving an "unresolved tension": "In the economic sphere it seemed the very image of progress, but in the arena of politics it had, in some measure, restored the old colonial order." The result was that the "internal tensions of the time . . . reached a new point of explosion."[19]

Krauze is describing Mexico in 1910, when the long dictatorship of Porfirio Díaz and the system he created were overturned by a social revolution, one hundred years after the first true revolution in the country. The massive rich-poor gap was, the Mexican historian Justo Serra writes, the "seed of the violent storms that were to come."[20] The question is whether the year 2005 or 2010 could, after a decade of worsening inequality and unemployment and alienation, bring about the same result. It seems highly unlikely, but as Jorge Castañeda has pointed out, "the dictator Porfirio Díaz remarked, as he sailed to exile in France in 1911, 'In Mexico nothing ever happens until it happens.' The country erupts sporadically and regionally because the inequities from which it suffers become at some point intolerable."[21] If things reach such a point in the next decade, social revolution, though unlikely, will be the result.

Colombianization

This subscenario involves the creation of a narcostate on the Colombian model. It assumes that current trends continue and that substantial portions of Mexican society come to be dominated by drug gangs. The implications of such a scenario are depressingly familiar: widespread social violence, including murder rates several times over those in other Latin American countries; the corrupting influences of drug gangs reaching into the upper echelons of the Mexican government and turning the entire state machinery to their benefit; and the assassination and intimidation of anyone—journalists, civic leaders, government lawyers—who stands in the way of the drug regime.

One disturbing but reliable indicator of this process is growing evidence that members of the Congress are taking money from drug traffickers. To date narcotraffickers have largely targeted Mexican judges; until recently, Congress was a rubber-stamp institution, and the drug gangs apparently believed that they did not have to buy off its members. Now they may feel they have to.

Of all the subscenarios of "Ungovernability," this is the one that appears to be the furthest developed. Drug shipments into the United States have reached an unprecedented volume; Mexico has begun to generate its own drug kingpins, operating independently of (and often in competition with) counterparts in Colombia and elsewhere; and violence is regularly directed at journalists and government officials attempting to expose the trend. Moreover, amid recent reports that Mexican-U.S. cooperative anti-drug operations have been an abject failure, there is little sense about where an effective response to this accelerating trend might be found.

The Colombianization of Mexico need not involve a collapse of social order. One can imagine a version of this scenario in which crime rates within Mexico City actually *decline* as the drug bosses win public sympathy. Moreover, the scenario is likely to involve a tight network of actual drug barons along with businessmen, government officials, and military leaders, so that economic development can actually proceed at a good pace in many areas of the country. The facade of a stable, even representative, government could remain in place; a social contract would seem to be operating. But the country will be run to serve the interests of a rich and corrupt few, and in the long run social stability is almost certain to suffer.

Exacerbating whatever domestic social strains arise in a Mexican narcostate is the immense hostility that would inevitably arise abroad, especially in Mexico's relations with the United States and many nations of Central and South America. Washington will no doubt take a very tough line, perhaps going as far as to revoke NAFTA and take extreme measures to halt all legal and illegal immigration. Given Mexico's economic dependence on the United States, such moves will destabilize Mexican society and perhaps lead to social chaos and even civil war.

Indicators of Scenario Five: Ungovernability

The specific combination of indicators that occurs will depend on which subscenario begins to emerge. They do not all go together.

- Social violence by all actors—guerrillas, vigilante groups, criminal gangs, narcotraffickers, paramilitary organizations, and military and police forces—increases substantially.

- Political participation is discredited and declines (except, perhaps, for protests and violent opposition to the government or ruling groups).

- Decentralization in government decisionmaking accelerates in a rapid but haphazard fashion.

- Survey results and psychological studies show severe disenchantment with society and politics, alienation, declining intersocial trust, and a growing incidence of psychological illness.

- Media sensationalism accelerates. Media influence fragments among various social interest groups.

- Illegal immigration to the United States surges, along with requests for political asylum.

- Reports of drug-related influence and activities grow as narcotraffickers increase their influence in the government, especially the Congress. There is growing evidence of corrupt ties between drug groups and the military. Paradoxically, there are also possibly increased reports of U.S.-Mexican counterdrug cooperation as the United States intervenes to keep this trend under control.

- There are growing reports of lack of governmental control over large areas of the country.

- Scores of new reports of government corruption surface, at first from within Mexico and then, increasingly, from media sources outside the country.

- Severe regional strains disrupt the political system. PAN and PDR remain regional parties, and northern cities and states refuse to pay taxes to central government.

- Foreign direct investment and tourism plummet. Those foreign investors who remain must deal with regional bosses, drug kingpins, and other nongovernmental authorities.

- Economic growth stagnates and declines, nationally or in specific regions, due to declining investment. Unemployment rises.

- The informal sector of the economy, if it includes the drug trade, increases its proportion of the nation's employment.

- Power is shared among several public and private actors, from governors to business to the church and the federal government.

- Corporate leaders are increasingly tied to government corruption schemes and narcotraffickers. Reports increase of repressive activities by corporations trying to "rule" parts of the country.

- Protests against the government are staged by workers, the poor, and Indians in the south and southeast.

- Environmental protection declines. Tensions with the United States on environmental issues grow.

- Rebel groups increase their operations and begin targeting the capital and other key sites.

- Regionally, Mexico's relations with all its neighbors suffer as outside actors attempt to press for reform, social control, and political freedom.

Notes

1. Similar scenario-building exercises have been undertaken in the past. One of the best and most recent is Gerardo Otero, "Mexico's Economic and Political Futures," in Gerardo Otero, ed., *Neoliberalism Revisited: Economic Restructuring and Mexico's Political Future* (Boulder, Colo.: Westview Press, 1996), 233–245. Subsequent endnotes refer to some of Otero's scenarios when they relate to scenarios being proposed here.

2. Gerardo Otero has similarly defined a "liberal democracy" scenario as one that combines grassroots democracy with market-led economics; Otero, "Mexico's Economic and Political Futures," 239.

3. Samuel Huntington, *Political Order in Changing Societies* (New Haven: Yale University Press, 1968).

4. Sergio Sarmiento, "Mexico's Inevitable Transformation," *Washington Quarterly* 20, no. 4 (Autumn 1997): 139.

5. Jorge G. Castañeda, "Ferocious Differences," *Atlantic*, July 1995, 9; available at <www.theatlantic.com>.

6. Otero, "Mexico's Economic and Political Futures," 241.

7. Nicholas Wilson, "What's Wrong with This Picture?" *Business Mexico*, April 1997, 23.
8. Otero, "Mexico's Economic and Political Futures," 239–242.
9. Enrique Krauze, *Mexico: Biography of Power*, trans. Hank Heifetz (New York: HarperCollins, 1997), 796.
10. Andrew Reding, "Facing Political Reality," *Washington Quarterly* 20, no. 4 (Autumn 1997): 108.
11. Patrick Oster, *The Mexicans: A Personal Portrait of a People* (New York: Harper and Row, 1989), 286–287.
12. Michael Radu, "The Looming Mexican Crisis," *Washington Quarterly* 20, no. 4 (Autumn 1997): 120–21.
13. Ibid., 126.
14. Krauze, *Mexico: Biography of Power*, 88.
15. Carlos Fuentes, *A New Time for Mexico* (Berkeley: University of California Press, 1996), 204.
16. Robert D. Kaplan, "History Moving North," *Atlantic*, February 1997, 21-22, 24. Otero has a scenario called "savage capitalism" involving a military-technocrat alliance favoring business interests, which shares some aspects in common with the uncontrolled corporate power aspects of our scenario; Otero, "Mexico's Economic and Political Futures," 240.
17. Fuentes, *A New Time for Mexico*, 111.
18. Octavio Paz, *The Labyrinth of Solitude and Other Writings*, trans. Lysander Kemp, Yara Milos, and Rachel Phillips Belash (New York: Grove Press, 1985), 270–272.
19. Krauze, *Mexico: Biography of Power*, 22.
20. Cited in Krauze, *Mexico: Biography of Power*, 220.
21. Castañeda, "Ferocious Differences," 5.

8 ■
The Knowledge Era and Mexico

> "There is nothing more difficult to take in hand, more perilous to conduct, or more uncertain in its success than to take the lead in the introduction of a new order of things."
>
> — Niccolò Machiavelli, *The Prince*

THE OVERALL GLOBAL TRENDS research effort, of which this country study is one element, comes to the broad conclusion that the promise embodied in many aspects of the knowledge era warrants a cautious optimism about developments over the coming decade. The dominant trends of the knowledge era are hopeful: empowering, democratizing, egalitarian, and environmentally healthy. But the dangers inherent in this era—and in the forms that reactions to change and the byproducts of these trends can take—demand caution. Optimism stems from the fact that the knowledge era provides the information, social institutions, and technologies needed to make the right choices; caution is rooted in an uncertainty that, even with the ability and the knowledge, the right choices will actually be made. The effort to shape this transformation so that it works for good rather than ill demands new social institutions, new values, new authorities.

The three most important aspects of this transition are the decisive role of education, as the activity that equips people for success in the knowledge era; the primacy of moral values and social responsibility, at a time when both must play a role in dealing with social ills; and the need for a "renewed capitalism," a reform of elements of capitalist systems to ensure that markets capture the true costs and implications of economic activities. Together, these factors define the social and economic agenda of the next decade. How well the nations and peoples of the world, including Mexico, tackle that agenda will determine whether our optimism or our caution proves out.

Over the next decade, Mexico will continue to learn the truth of Machiavelli's insight into "the introduction of a new order of things" during what is arguably the most fundamental social transition in that country's history. The country enjoys a remarkable opportunity to build a new economy, a new society, and a new politics, all of which can empower and enrich its people as never before. Yet to achieve that hopeful future Mexico must surmount a host of intense challenges in every area of public policy. It is not clear whether Mexico is up to the task—or whether the United States is up to the parallel challenge of playing a mature and constructive role in the bilateral relationship, a role of great importance for Mexico's future.

In particular, the case of Mexico underscores the importance of the three necessary areas of response to the demands of the knowledge era: education, reformed capitalism, and a renewed sense of public moral values.

A number of trends emphasize the importance of improved education in Mexico and the weakness of the current system. Not only is the primary and secondary educational system overloaded; it is also deficient. Only 60 percent of children aged 5 to 11 complete their primary education; secondary attendance is also low—about 4.7 million students in 1995-1996, compared to nearly 15 million in primary school. The attendance rate for higher education is a mere 1,500 per 100,000 population, compared to more than 5,000 in both the United States and Canada.[1] In the 1996-1997 school year, only 1.6 million Mexican students were enrolled in higher education, up from 1.35 million in 1994. Graduate-level enrollment reached 108,000 by 1997, an increase from 66,000 in 1994.[2]

Just how far Mexico has to go is captured by the simple fact that the average Mexican has just seven years of education, up from three in the early 1970s.[3] Apart from these quantitative problems, there are qualitative ones as well:

> Teaching conditions at the primary and secondary levels are generally poor. Most classrooms in the country have over forty children per teacher. A single teacher is frequently responsible for as many as six grades. Many schools do not extend over the full six or twelve years. Teachers are often very young and poorly trained,

and are sometimes not even available in many areas of the country.[4]

Rays of hope exist: according to the Office of the President in Mexico City, the percentage of children beginning primary school who go on to finish sixth grade has climbed from 74 percent in 1993-1994 to 83 percent in 1997-1998 and is expected to reach almost 90 percent by 2001.[5] The Mexican government, nongovernmental organizations, corporations, and civic leaders must work to consolidate this improvement over the coming decade.

Solutions to the problems in higher education are closely connected to economic questions. There are simply not enough white-collar jobs, even for the relatively small number of college graduates being produced today. One estimate suggests that in the 1980s, Mexican universities turned out more than 1.3 million graduates, but the economy generated only 311,000 new professional jobs.[6]

These numbers reinforce an important message of the preceding chapters: solutions to social and economic problems are closely intertwined.

One implication of this fact is the need, in Mexico as throughout the world, for new thinking on the ways in which capitalism can be modified or reformed to meet social needs. Carlos Fuentes has spoken of the need to "reconcile growth and justice," to develop an "inclusive modernity"; Octavio Paz has warned that, while it was at first "imperative to achieve economic progress," now "for this progress to continue, it is equally imperative to achieve social development—that is, justice."[7] Both of these perspectives reflect the global challenge of moderating the impact of liberal economics.

One of the most important arguments of the first Global Trends 2005 Study is that capitalism, newly triumphant over socialism and statism of all kinds, cannot sit back and smugly assume that its victory is unconditional or permanent. In its pure and untempered form, free-market capitalism does not nurture values such as community, mercy, ecology, equality, or justice. These values are injected into capitalist systems by human institutions and moral values. This is no longer a partisan view, if it ever was; in the United States, social conservatives worried about the state of moral values, communities, and families now point just as urgently to the need for nonmarket social ethics as do more traditional critics of capitalism on the left. If the end of the Cold War and the wave of liberalization sweeping through the developing world are to be sustained, capitalist systems will need to expend greater—not less—effort over the coming decade to keep other human, social, and environmental values in mind.

Two areas in which a more humane version of capitalism will be especially important in Mexico are social equity and the environment. As the country progresses economically, it must ensure that the benefits of progress are shared throughout the society, not captured by a wealthy few. This will not happen naturally, but it cannot be imposed by a new socialist system, which would merely deny progress to all. Mexico, like many other countries at a similar stage of development, must find ways of improving social and economic equality—and, it should be reemphasized, environmental sustainability and health—without resorting to statism.

These recommendations have a certain poignancy in the context of the debate over the origins and impact of Mexico's liberalization drive. As Miguel Centeno and others have documented, while many of the liberal technocrats of the 1980s and 1990s did appear to have the best interests of average Mexicans at heart, the liberal economic program—like so many others in the industrial and developing world, from Ronald Reagan's and Margaret Thatcher's plans to the post-communist reforms in eastern Europe—did not include strategies for addressing social concerns. If future Mexican governments expect to press ahead with liberalization without generating a widespread backlash, this void needs to be filled.

It must be filled in part by a growing reference to the role of moral and spiritual values in public policy. The worldwide trend in this direction is evident, and Mexico boasts a long history of drawing ethical concerns into public policy—at least in rhetoric. José María Morelos y Pavón, a leader of the 1810 revolution, laid out the set of values that guided his actions:

> I would like us to make the declaration that there is no nobility but that of virtue, knowledge, patriotism and charity; that we are all equal, since we all come from the same origin, . . . that the children of the peasant and the sweeper should have the same edu-

cation as the children of the rich hacendado; that every just claimant should have access to a court which listens, protects and defends him against the strong and the arbitrary . . . [that the laws should be] such that they . . . narrow the gap between wealth and poverty and increase the daily wages of the poor.[8]

It would be difficult to imagine a better summary of the kind of basic principles needed today. Many of the wrenching decisions mandated by the knowledge era require moral and ethical as well as political perspectives. Without a vigorous sense of the values underpinning public policy, it is not clear that the right decisions can be made.

These three ingredients—education, a reformed and renewed capitalism, and an increasing reliance on moral values—can nourish Mexico through the turbulent transition ahead. It has been and remains difficult to be optimistic about Mexico, given the country's daunting array of economic, social, environmental, and political challenges. If one looks closely enough, though, a few signs of a more promising future do reveal themselves. One writer has described the country as

> shedding its skin, the one it couldn't fit into any longer. If we're optimistic we see a democratic Mexico—culturally, spiritually and politically—being born. A new era of *mestizaje*, a negotiation between old and new.

If we are less hopeful we see

> another Mexico, one whose crisis is so severe that it is tearing itself apart and may never come back together again. . . . Sound like any of a few dozen other places on the globe? Yes. Mexico is very much a part of the present, even though outsiders usually see only its past.[9]

The collision between these two eras—the passing industrial age and the onrushing knowledge era—will continue to reshape Mexican society, economics, politics, and psychology over the next decade. The opportunity exists to use this shock to fashion a prosperous, empowered, hopeful society. The only question is what future Mexico and the Mexicans choose for themselves.

Notes

1. Economist Intelligence Unit, *Mexico 1996–1997*, 20.
2. "About Mexico," INEGI homepage at <www.inegi.gob.mx>); Ernesto Zedillo, "The Nation: Progress and Challenges," Third State of the Nation Address, September 1, 1997, available at <www.presidencia.gob.mx>.
3. Sergio Sarmiento, "Mexico's Inevitable Transformation," *Washington Quarterly* 20, no. 4 (Autumn 1997): 134.
4. David E. Lorey, "Education and the Challenges of Mexican Development," *Challenge* 38, no. 2 (1995): 51.
5. Available at <www.presidencia.gob.mx> under "Social Statistics."
6. Lorey, "Education and the Challenges of Mexican Development."
7. Octavio Paz, *The Labyrinth of Solitude and Other Writings*, trans. Lysander Kemp, Yara Milos, and Rachel Phillips Belash (New York: Grove Press, 1985), 259–260.
8. Cited in Enrique Krauze, *Mexico: Biography of Power*, trans. Hank Heifetz (New York: HarperCollins, 1997), 112.
9. Ruben Martinez, "Mexico's Search for Itself: Cultural Change in Mexico," *The Nation*, April 28, 1997, 22.

Index

Afores. *See* Pension fund companies (afores).
Alienation: in Mexico, 126–131; problems of, 121–123
Anxiety, 119–120
Authority: crime as indicator of changes in, 102–103; crisis of, 93–94; factors in weakening of social, 94–95; knowledge-era, 96; in knowledge era, 93–94; rise of new, 95, 97; transformation in Mexico, 98, 106–115
Authority, nongovernmental: business as, 113; nongovernmental organizations as, 109–110; religion as, 110–111, 113
Awareness, global, 74, 81
Banking sector: effects of financial crisis on, 39, 61–62; in Mexican SME market, 58; post-1994/1995 financial crisis, 61–62; proposals for, 60; weakness of, 58
Basañez, Miguel, 24, 35, 36, 41, 80, 82, 99–100
Border, U.S.-Mexican: economic development along, 54; tensions, 79

Branden, Nathaniel, 119
Business sector: role in environmental protection, 113; strategy in knowledge era, 112; strategy in Mexico, 112
Capitalism: need for renewed, 165; values of free-market, 167–168
Capital markets: capital scarcity for Mexican SMEs, 58; effect of pension reform on, 62–63; in human resources economy, 49; with privatized retirement savings, 62
Càrdenas, Cuauhtémoc, 36, 107
Castañeda, Jorge, xvi, 64, 82–83, 139
Catholic Church, 110, 113
Centeno, Miguel, 168
Central bank, Mexico, 108
Chiapas state, 106
Communication technologies, global, 75
Competition: in knowledge era, 47; with networked organizations, 48–49
Competitiveness: of Mexican SMEs, 57–58; of service sector firms, 59

Congress, Mexico, 107
Corruption: in Mexico, 101; in nondemocratic systems, 101
Counterglobalism, 33
Covey Leadership Center, Mexico, 112
Crime, Mexico, 102–103
Culture: influence on world trends, 7; Mexican, 22–24
Decentralization: effect on distribution of power, 88, 108–109; of government power, 84–85, 87; of knowledge-era authorities, 96; of management decisionmaking, 96
Democracy: advance of (1800s–2005), 34; effect on civil society of emerging, 110; emergence in Mexico, xviii, xx, 35–37; indicators of Mexico as, 140–142; transition to, 137
Demography trends in Mexico, 7–9, 52
Drucker, Peter, xv, 95
Drug traffic or narcotrafficking, 103–105
Earthquake potential in Mexico, 10
Economic growth: in developing world, 51–52; Mexico's future potential, 9, 11; potential for Mexico with, 52; role in Mexico, 66, 68; U.S.-Mexican border development, 54
Economic policy: effect on civil society of liberalized, 110; liberalization of, 38–40; privatization of state-owned enterprises, 39–40
Economic power shift, 51–52
The Economist, 40
Education: importance in Mexico, 131–132; importance of improved, 166–167; of knowledge-era worker, 48; role in knowledge era, 165
Ejército Revolucionario Popular (ERP), 106
Electoral system reforms, Mexico, 36
Energy, renewable: potential for, 6; technology for, 30
Energy demand, Mexico, 21–22
Environmental issues: developing and industrial worlds, 3–4; Mexico, 12–14, 16–17; role of business in, 113
Evangelical Protestant movement, 111
Exports: growth and share of, 55f, 56f; *maquiladora* products as, 54; from Mexican and foreign firms in Mexico, 56; oil, 54
Family, the: decay of, 94; family values in Mexico, 87, 100; Mexican, 128–129
Federal Electricity Commission, Mexico, 39
Financial sector: crisis (1994–1995), 39, 61, 68; need to liberalize Mexico's, 59, 61; weaknesses of, 69
Firms, virtual, 47–48
Foreign direct investment (FDI): in Mexico, 55, 57
Fuentes, Carlos, 41, 66, 68, 86, 108, 110, 130–131, 167
Fukuyama, Francis, 33
Gerstner, Louis, 76
Globalism: pluralism within, 87, 89
Globalization: effect in Mexico, 63–64, 78, 80, 83–84; engines of, 78, 80–81; process of, 73–75; role of multinational companies in, 75
Glynn, Patrick, 76

Government, Mexico: Energy
   Secretariat, 21; environmental
   program, 15
Hamel, Gary, 95
Havel, Vaclav, xviii
Heath, Jonathan, 59, 65
Hegel, Georg, 33
Hierarchy: as concept in business,
   112
Human beings: as authority in
   knowledge era, 97; needs, desires,
   and aspirations of, 31–32
Humboldt, Alexander von, 63
Huntington, Samuel, 78, 87, 138
Immigration, illegal, 67
Income distribution: in knowledge
   era, 50–51; in Mexico, 63–64,
   66, 68
Industrial era: knowledge era as shift
   from, xv–xvi; problems of, xv–xvi
Industrial sector: use of modern
   production technology, 56
Industrial sector, Mexico: employment in *maquiladora* industries,
   54–55; exports of *maquiladora*
   industry, 54
Inequality, socioeconomic: effect of
   globalization on, 83; in Mexico,
   63–65
Informal sector: employment in, 54;
   microbusinesses in, 58
Information: in knowledge era, xviii;
   provided by knowledge era, 165;
   technology related to, 30–31
Inglehart, Ronald, 24, 35, 36, 41,
   80, 99–100
Innovation in knowledge era, 96
Institutional Revolutionary Party
   (PRI): effect of electoral defeat
   of, 110, 113; erosion of power of,
   98–99; reduced influence of, 107;
   with reformed electoral system, 36
Institutions: decline in strength of,
   93; decline of influence of social,
   102; emergence in Mexico of,
   106–115; emerging in Mexico,
   98; in knowledge era, 96;
   provided by knowledge era, 165;
   to support democracy in Mexico,
   37; virtual state as new, 95
Insurgent movements, 104, 106
Jones, James, 149
Kaplan, Robert, 9
Kierkegaard, Sören, 120
Knowledge: effect on authority, 94;
   role in creation of wealth, 45
Knowledge era: characteristics of,
   xviii, xxiii; dangers of demagoguery, 123; dominant trends of,
   165; effect of principles of, 48;
   Mexico as member of, 81, 129–
   130; networked entities of, 46,
   48–49; pluralism of, 75–77; role
   of authority in, 94–95, 97;
   science and technology in, 29–
   31; services sector in, 59; shift
   from industrial-era society to, xv,
   xviii; virtual organizations of, 47;
   at work in Mexico, 63
Krauze, Enrique, xx, 35, 109
Labor force: employment growth in
   Mexico, 9, 11; in knowledge era,
   47–48
Machiavelli, Niccolò, 165
Manufacturing sector: characteristics
   of current, 54, 56; downsizing in
   (1990–1996), 59; use of technology in, 56
May, Rollo, 120
Media, the: characteristics of
   Mexican, 131; negative and
   pessimistic reporting, 122
Mexico: as country in transition, xvi;

Mexico *(continued)*
  evolving economy of, xvi; indicators of democracy in, 140–142; indicators of losing ground, 146–149; indicators of old ideas redesigned, 151–153; indicators of status quo in, 144; indicators of ungovernability, 160–162; integration with United States, 82; themes related to future of, xvii–xviii, xx–xxi, xxiii
Meyrowitz, Joshua, 121
Military sector, 109
Mobility: effect of increased, 94
Modernization, socioeconomic, 31–32
Moore, James, 48, 97
Morelos y Pavón, José Maria, 168–169
Multinational companies: adjustment to Mexican cultural standards, 87; increased number of, 75
National Action Party (PAN): decentralization agenda, 84–85; growing influence of, 107–108; with reformed electoral system, 36
Nationalism, Mexican, 80, 82
Nation-state: as present-day authority, 95; weakened role of, 100
Nevitte, Neil, 24, 35, 36, 41, 80, 99–100
Nongovernmental organizations: rising role and number of, 109; in social sector, 95
North American Free Trade Agreement (NAFTA): in regional social contract, 40–41
O'Grady, Shawna, 112
Oppenheimer, Andres, 61, 82
Organizations, virtual, 47

Party of the Democratic Revolution (PRD): national party goals, 85; perceived philosophy of, 107–108; with reformed electoral system, 36
Paz, Octavio, xx, 23, 63, 66, 87, 114, 167
Pemex: as state-owned enterprise, 39–40
Pension fund companies *(afores)*, 62–63
Pension system, 58–59
Pessimism, 122, 124–125
Pluralism: within globalism, 87, 89; of knowledge era, 75–77; rise in Mexico, 84–85, 87
Political parties: in knowledge era, 99; PAN-PRD competition, 85
Political system: corruption in Mexico's, 58
Population: aging of Mexican, 8–9; growth in developing and industrialized world, 2–3, 5; growth in Mexico, 8, 12
Postmaterialism, Mexican, 80–81
Poverty, Mexico, 65–66
Prices: potential spikes in commodity prices, 5–6
Privatization: politics of, 40; during Zedillo regime, 39–40
Protestantism, 111
Regionalism: in Mexico, 84–85, 87
Religion: Evangelical movement, 111; as nongovernmental authority, 110, 113
Research and development (R&D): government-led and private, 56
Resources, natural: petroleum, 19–21; prices of commodities from, 5–6; water sources in Mexico, 17–19

Rule of law: in Mexico, 97; requirements related to, 40
Samuelson, Robert, 124
Sarmiento, Sergio, 138–139
Sennett, Richard, 94
Services sector, Mexico, 59
Small and medium-sized enterprises (SMEs): needed improvement for, 57–58; in service sector, 59–60
SMEs. *See* Small and medium-sized enterprises (SMEs).
Social construction, 32
Social contract, global, 40
Social insurance: pension system reform, 62–63, 69
Social sector, nonprofit, 95
Social security system, 9, 11
Society: inequality in, 63–66; middle class as minority in, 64, 68; weakened civil, 94
Society, civil: emergence of fuller, 109–110; shift in Mexico to diversified, 98
State-owned enterprises (SOEs): privatized and yet-to-be privatized, 39–40
Stresses, psychological: in Mexico, 125–131

Technology: global communication, 75; in knowledge era, 29–31; provided by knowledge era, 165; used in business and manufacturing sectors, 56
Trade: growth of global, 73–74; of Mexico with United States, 82
Tribalism, 75–76; within globalism, 76, 78; rise in Mexico, 84–85, 87
Trust: lacking in business relationships, 112
Universalism, 76
Urbanization: in developing world, 2; in Mexico, 11, 100
van Delden, Maarten, 86
Vargas Llosa, Mario, 35
Virtual state, 95
Weintraub, Sidney, 98
Whitehead, Alfred North, xv
Work ethic, Mexican, 112
Wright, Jeff, 113
Wriston, Walter, 45, 96
Zapatista National Liberation Army, 106
Zedillo, Ernesto, 39, 102

About the Author

MICHAEL J. MAZARR is editor of the *Washington Quarterly*, director of the New Millennium Project, and dean of the Young Leaders Program at the Center for Strategic and International Studies in Washington, D.C. Dr. Mazarr holds B.A. and M.A. degrees from Georgetown University, in government and national security studies, and a Ph.D. in policy analysis from the University of Maryland School of Public Affairs.

Dr. Mazarr is also an adjunct professor at Georgetown University, where he teaches international politics. He has been a U.S. Naval Reserve intelligence officer, a term member of the Council on Foreign Relations, and a founding member of both the Council on Security Cooperation in the Asia-Pacific (CSCAP) and the Committee on Nuclear Policy. He is a member of the International Institute for Strategic Studies (IISS) and a visiting faculty fellow at Penn State University's Schreyer Honors College. From 1993 to 1995, he was legislative assistant for foreign affairs and chief writer in the office of Representative Dave McCurdy (D-Okla.).

Dr. Mazarr has authored eight books, including *Semper Fidel: America and Cuba, 1776–1988* (1988), *START and the Future of Deterrence* (1990), and *North Korea and the Bomb: A Case Study in Nonproliferation* (1995). His latest work, *Global Trends 2005: An Owner's Manual for the Next Decade*, will be published as a trade book by St. Martin's Press in 1999.